ANGER MANAGEMENT

HOW TO STOP LOSING CONTROL, GUIDE YOUR EMOTIONS, AND BUILD EMOTIONAL INTELLIGENCE

RUBY DANIELS

CONTENTS

She tells me the news she has been so terrified to tell me and everything turns red. Then black, now red again. I feel the droplets of sweat beginning to form on my brow as my jaw clenches in an iron hold. I am almost *willing* my blood pressure to rise as the pounding of my own pulse beats hard against my ears. Cue the tremors, slight at first, now uncontrollable, my body could almost split the earth beneath it. And so here I stand, a shaking unshakeable volcano, eruption imminent and, when it comes, deadly to those around it. She tells me that my eyes have turned almost completely black, which makes sense as I can virtually feel the blood rushing at lightning speed through my veins. As for my vision itself, I am looking ahead but I cannot see. It's as though everything is unrecognizable, everything except the blinding rage that's bursting within me, and soon without me. The objects that surround me skew to a blur, and her voice is a dull echo beneath the waves of emotion and adrenaline that crash against my skull and chest. Time seems non-existent, and in that moment I do not remember ever feeling anything else. And it has, indeed, been only a moment. The time arrives for me to behave in a way that is unrecognizable to my rational self, to create another storm, the damage of which I will never really be able to take back. It's the second time this week, and it's only Wednesday.

That is what's so difficult about this, isn't it? How do you begin to control something that your mind and body fall victim to *so* intensely in a matter of seconds? It feels like being asked to alter the future whilst being frozen in the present... or, more often than not, the past. But that's my story, and no two human beings on this planet are the same, thank goodness. Perhaps you're not the type that boils over at a single word, that hurtles objects at walls, throws fists through mirrors or is deafened by the shrill sound of your own shrieking voice. Perhaps you're a ticking timebomb—the type that bottles it up and pockets the feelings in the few spaces you have left in the far corners of your soul. Well, time will continue to pass, and blank emotionless spaces will eventually yield to become colored until there is nowhere else to turn. Perhaps you don't wear your scars on your face and keep them locked away in your heart... perhaps anger doesn't even appear in your life as an apparent problem. I've lost count of the times I've heard myself say, *"but I don't even feel angry"* in the beginning. Maybe you don't either. But, are you lonely? Anxious? Afraid? Ashamed? Anger has many faces, but no mask is eternal. The trick is to try and unveil it before it becomes your own reflection in the mirror.

SLOW DOWN

When it comes to controlling our emotions, improving our emotional intelligence, growing spiritually or however you want to phrase it, the biggest problem is that everyone, everywhere in the world is in such a rush. In my humble experience on this planet, it is the things that we want to resolve the quickest that take the most time, and how *frustrating* it is! I know you've probably heard this many times already but here is a solid, unchanging and brutal fact: quick fixes **do not work.** Take weight loss, for example—or heartbreak! How many times have we tried to meet the far-fetched expectations of the perfect media body by eating far less and, in my experience, smoking far more, only to pile it all back on the next month? How many french martinis, sticky dancefloors, rom-coms and never-ending tubs of ice cream have we substituted for simply letting ourselves feel lonely, rejected, heartbroken? In the end, rushing to the finish line often makes the race last a lot longer, and when you're only really competing with yourself, what's the point?

And so, one of the most important themes I would like to highlight from the very beginning, and one that you should keep in your life's pocket in any given situation is this: take your time. What's the rush? Growing spiritually, controlling our anger, however it may present itself, and building emotional intelligence sound like profound, perhaps even daunting tasks, at first glance. However, they are no different to losing a few pounds, getting over a partner who was never right for you anyway, or simply watering the sunflowers in your back garden. Life, including all its weirdness and misdirection, is a process. We all want to speed up the bad and bathe in the good, but the bad is, unfortunately, often where we learn the most about ourselves. At the end of the day, whether you choose to take this advice or not, it will be forced upon you. No mortal can speed up or slow down the passage of time, no one can click their fingers and suddenly reach nirvana. So, if we are to be stuck in this gruelling process that all of us want to complete but none of us really know how, we may as well be aware of it. It is not a shameful thing to feel disharmony within yourself, nor to struggle with emotional control, nor to have no idea where to begin making changes. The same way it is not shameful to experience heartbreak, or forget to water your flowers. The first step in any form of growth is realizing you have *room* to grow. You are already on the path to becoming better. So take your time, allow yourself to feel and cut yourself some slack. With a sprinkle of the waters of knowledge, the perseverance to withstand the winds of hardship and the welcoming of the new life from the sun, my goodness, like the flowers, you will shine. If you are already able to live in each moment, allowing all the feelings in it to wash over you, whilst separating it from yourself and giving it the time and energy that it is indeed due, you can stop reading now... and you can let me know how.

The Every-Day

Taking the aforementioned into consideration, it is important to note that not all situations where we struggle to control our anger result in furious outbursts or earth-shattering arguments that alter our relationships beyond repair. Recognizing that we may need help with emotional control might creep up on us during the most mundane of tasks. For example, when we are standing silently in a supermarket queue that just won't move, or miss the subway by five small seconds and have to wait five agonizing minutes for the next one when we are already late. It may be the warm swell in our stomachs when the idiot driver cuts in front of us without signalling, or the sharpness of our tongues when an innocent bystander accidentally bumps into us on the crowded street. Granted, these situations would cause most people a slight inconvenience, but if you have chosen to read this book, my guess is that, like me, you can tell the difference between feeling slightly inconvenienced and utterly enraged, for several minutes or even hours after it should've subsided, I might add.

First of all, you are not alone. You would be surprised at the vast number of people who struggle immensely to control their emotions. And who can blame us? After all, when are we taught it? I don't remember being told how to rationalize situations in real-time or how to breathe properly and calmly when I was in school. I have zero recollection of being helped to understand that my anger did not define me, and could be dealt with by visiting my past rather than visiting the headmaster's office. Education is, of course, a vital part of our lives, but I can't lie and say I was ever educated much about life. We are left to unravel these mysteries for ourselves, often without support or guidance and often already pretty damaged. For a while, I blamed my parents. And yes, as a parent it is your job to try to help and guide your children as much as possible. But as I grew up, my parents turned from superheroes to just... people. Like you and me, still trying to find their *own* way in the world whilst carrying the burden of paving my way too. No, it is our own job as individuals to strive to do better. The good news is, though we are all on different paths, we seek the same thing, and by nature, are bound together and supported by one another. These modest few chapters of advice and experience are designed to help you to understand that fact, and know that there is *always* room to grow. You have taken the first step by picking it up.

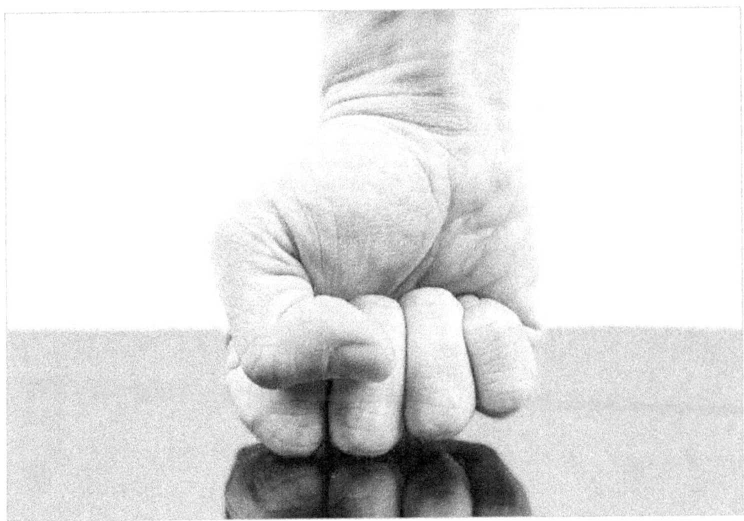

1

HELLO, ANGER

Whoever you are, wherever you are, whatever gender, age, sexuality or race, you know what it means to feel anger. For many it comes in the form of a blinding rage that seems uncontrollable, accompanied by a heartbeat like a fast jungle drum, that horrible churning sensation in your stomach and a tension so tight across your whole body that your head begins to ache. If you experience this you can also expect to feel the sticky sickening sweat that spreads across your forehead and palms, and the utter inability to control, or keep up with, any of your racing thoughts. For others, anger is a silent arch-nemesis, never allowed out but always there, waiting to be provoked and on the verge of explosion. Some people deal with anger in a healthy, simple way and know exactly how to put it in its place. Lucky them. Whichever way you choose to deal with anger is your business, however it is here that a certain quote by Eckhart

Tolle springs to mind, a quote that made me re-evaluate the entirety of how I coped with my emotions: *"Where there is anger, there is always pain underneath."* Anger, like all emotions, does not discriminate between the different types of people that it affects. However, it does stand out from other emotions in its fierce intensity, and the consequences that come with it. You say things you wish you hadn't, do things you wish you could undo, and the ripple effect can take a long time to settle down. Following anger, people often feel shame, self-loathing and regret. Anger is seen as an unattractive, malicious emotion and something that we really should try to avoid. But, as so beautifully put by spiritual teacher Eckhart Tolle, our anger is the consequence of some sort of other pain in our lives —it is not something to be ashamed of and it is *certainly* not something to ever be avoided. Another preliminary issue I would like to address here is the way anger is perceived in terms of gender. Looking around in recent years, it seems to me that anger is unladylike and irrational in women, but a sign of strength and masculinity in men. I find both these ideas problematic beyond words. In short, anger is a sign of mental disharmony and a disruption within us. It is not irrational or unattractive, nor is it something to be praised and glorified. It is an emotion often brought on from some form of trauma or distress in our lives, and it is something we must learn to confront and control. Do not be mistaken in thinking you are right or wrong to feel anger—it is a naturally occurring emotion and, like everything else in life, needs to be balanced.

As previously mentioned, anger can take many different forms and present itself differently according to who is feeling it. It is important to note that anger should not actually be considered a "bad" emotion. Of course, when given the choice I am sure most of us would choose to feel joy, excitement and happiness over despair, sadness or grief, but life would be too boring if that was the case. We are tinted by the colors of every emotion on the spectrum, and whether we like it or not, they all demand to be felt at some point in our lives. This, of course, is a good thing in the end. If we were happy and carefree all the time, how would we ever learn to cope with darkness? With loss and hurt? How would we ever acquire the skills to advise our loved ones when *they* find themselves in a bad place? Similarly, without that aching darkness that each one of us dreads, how would we ever know true happiness? Or what it means to love and to be loved? We are all walking balances of this sliding scale, and it takes a while, sometimes a lifetime, to find a happy middle. Anger has its place too—for me, it sits at the head of the table. Yes, anger can have negative effects on ourselves and those around us, yes it can be an unpleasant emotion to physically feel, but it can be used for good. The same way a great wave of sorrow can be used to create the most heart-wrenching piece of poetry, for example, anger can be used to tap into sides of ourselves we didn't even know *existed*. We can use the adrenaline to express ourselves creatively, fight our way through difficult situations, keep ourselves safe and force ourselves to push through to the end. This, however, cannot be achieved when anger sits at the head of the table. Nor when joy, sadness, anxiety, love or fear sit at the head of the table. Think of your emotions not as part of you, but as guests in your home. *You* sit at the head of the table, and *you* possess the intrinsic skills to move and control *your* emotions and their effects like pawns on a chessboard... you just don't know it yet.

THE CHEMISTRY OF ANGER

Like any issue or problem that is placed before us, in order to resolve it and/or control it, the most important thing to do is to identify where it comes from and how it works. When we can follow a chain of events to its source, it becomes easier to follow and understand. For anger, this works two-fold. As previously discussed, anger is usually a surface reaction for some sort of pain or issue that lies beneath it. Of course, sometimes we are angry just because. If we are wronged or hurt by someone, if someone is deliberately irritating us or even if we are just having an off day—you have the right to feel annoyed just because you feel annoyed. However, when anger is a recurring problem, it is a common consensus that there are other issues that need addressing, perhaps childhood trauma or mental disorders and so on and so forth. However, the idea of following something to its source is also important when dealing with anger in terms of the actual chemical make-up of the emotion in our brains. Understanding the chemistry of the way anger is produced in our brains can be massively beneficial in the way we react in the crucial moments during which it is at its peak. If we can understand that what is happening to us is a chemical process, one which we can actually learn to control, rather than a shameful, incomprehensible fragment of our being, we can begin to take the steps to recognize various parts of the process as they are happening and leave the shame behind. It is also useful in recognizing that everyone feels anger —it is not a unique hindrance to any one person, and though all of our brains are different, we possess the same parts that react to create the same process that results in each of us feeling anger. Try to remember that your emotions do not define you. Though it certainly doesn't feel like it a lot of the time, you are in control. You have all the tools within you to conquer your emotions and find inner peace, you just need to be shown how to use them!

Anger, first and foremost, is a response, perhaps to a trigger or a frustration, anxiety, fear or annoyance and so on. How we behave when we are angry depends on how our brains process this mental state. It is commonly known that there are two sides to our brains, we call these the left and right hemispheres. Many people actually sometimes characterize their personalities based on which side of the brain their character leans more toward. Though it is true that some people are more "left-brained" and some are more "right-brained," the two are equally as important as one another, and fulfill the needs of the body in different ways. The left brain is rational, predominantly concerned with logic, judgment and facts. The right brain, however, is associated with creativity, feelings and the imagination... I knew which category I fell under before the age of five. If, like me, you lean more toward the right side of your brain, the chances are you are more inclined to become over-emotional before even being presented with an issue. However, it does not stop there. Within the brain, there are many different systems which control various parts of our thought patterns and behaviors. The system that is concerned with our emotions is called the limbic system. In particular, we are going to play close attention to the amygdala, one of the most prominent structures in the brain that contributes to the make-up of the limbic system. This is the part that handles fear, activates anger and forces us into action. It is also the primary part of the brain that awakens our "fight or flight" response (Karmin, 2016). This refers to the kind of survival mode that kicks in when we are faced with a stressful and/or life-threatening situation. This part of the brain decides whether we stay to fight and face the situation head-on or whether we flee from it. So, as you can imagine, the amygdala has a considerable role to play when we are faced with feeling angry. When we feel anger, epinephrine, more commonly known as adrenaline, is released which causes things like an increased heart rate and our blood pressure to rise. At the same time, neurotransmitter chemicals are also released which cause similar reactions in the body as adrenaline.

Now, whilst the amygdala is busy warning you of an immediate threat and processing your anger, so is the prefrontal cortex, which lies at the very front of the brain. However, it is attacking the problem from the opposite angle. Whilst the amygdala focuses on primitive, instinctive reactions, the cortex judges things based on logic and reason. For example, if we are walking down the street at night and see a figure coming toward us, our amygdala sends warning signals out and adrenaline is automatically released. More often than not, the figure is harmless and there is actually no threat. Our prefrontal cortex is responsible for our decision to not start shouting and screaming for help, or accusing a poor dog-walker of being a danger… our amygdala is the reason we cross the road anyway. This interaction is the crucial moment in terms of how we behave when we become angry. If the reaction from the amygdala is overpowering, it will motivate the limbic system to react rather than the cortex—in other words, you will act emotionally rather than basing your reaction on reason and trying to decipher the logical way to act. This, in turn, leads people to behave in certain ways or say certain things that they normally wouldn't. The adrenaline rush we feel when our anger is at its peak is not just momentary and can last for many minutes, making it difficult to calm down and regain control once we have past the point. So, based on this information we can work something out. Can we completely eradicate an angry response from our system? Or suddenly become immune to anger? No. However, we can identify it as it is happening, and with this knowledge, we can possibly find it easier to try and rationalize our emotions before they get out of hand. This is, of course, easier said than done, but learning about the chemistry and make-up of anger in our brains is a huge step forward in learning how to control it. The brain reacts similarly when encountering stress, fear and anxiety. As previously mentioned, these emotions are often derived from, caused by or at least associated with feeling anger, so knowing this information can be helpful when dealing with these too.

Now that we can put the chemistry lesson aside, we can start to question the emotional side of anger. Are we *really* that annoyed because someone told us what to do? Can we *honestly* justify our reaction to missing that green light by a couple of seconds? More often than not, the answer is no. When our anger is a recurring issue that we feel slipping out of our grasp, it is far more likely that we have deeper issues to consider and face. However, we will tell ourselves that yes, we really were that annoyed at authority, and yes, anyone would be that mad about missing the lights. Why? Because we would often rather be kissed by a lie than slapped with the truth.

Why Are We So Angry?

Ah, what a question. It is my sincere hope that you will find at least some form of an answer after finishing this modest little book. This is a difficult question to pose, considering the fact that there are roughly seven billion people on the planet with each and every one being entirely different and leading separate lives. However, human beings are fundamentally tribal, and bound together by the very fact that we are human, so over the years we have uncovered some common causes of why we behave the way we do. The list of reasons that cause us to feel angry range from small, situational inconveniences to matters of life-changing, or indeed life-threatening seriousness. Sometimes, feeling angry can even transform these minor disturbances into something much more sinister. The problem with anger is that it comes in so many forms. It is the faceless stranger that lurks in the corner of our every-day and raises its gruesome head when we are at our most emotionally unstable. Anger is the person we become when we can take no more. So, we know where it comes from and how it forms in our brains, but what triggers this reaction? It really depends on the individual and their situation, but I urge you to consider that which you are about to read, and ask yourself if you recognize any parallels between it and your own life.

The funny thing about anger is that it is an emotion often brought on by other emotions, a consequential emotion, if you will. When we feel ashamed or embarrassed, anxious or hurt, we often bury these feelings in anger because these negative emotions are considered a danger or hazard to our overall well-being. As intelligent and complex as human beings are, we also have a raw, animalistic and innate sense of self-protection and self-defense. And so, when we begin to feel our delicate emotional walls becoming penetrated, we lash out, offend and attack in some vain effort to create some impregnable emotional fortress that will never really exist so long as we are human. With this in mind, can you think of anything in your life that's vexing you? Anything you don't want to deal with or even pretend isn't happening at all? This can range from problems at work, to struggles at home with children or family, relationship difficulties, friendship problems, or might even be an issue between you and yourself. If the answer is yes, the chances are this is linked to your anger.

Next up, we have the good old past that no one ever wants to revisit. This can often be the most confusing for people who are experiencing anger management issues, it was for me anyway. Many people reach a stage in their life where, on the surface, things actually finally seem ok. You might have a loving relationship, or a good job, a nice home or all three and more, but you're still angry. Cue self-loathing. How many *times* I have sat and racked my brain at what sort of horrible, ungrateful person I must be, because hey! My life is *good!* Why can't I be content? Why can't we all just move on? Unfortunately, that is not how life works. We can't just move on, we need to work on it. It is very common for people that experience problems with emotional control, especially in terms of their aggression, that they have suffered some sort of past trauma that they have not been able to fully process or recover from. This can range from abuse and violence, to neglect and addiction. I would like to mention here that it is important to allow yourself to feel how you feel. You may be reading this and thinking the classic, *"well what happened to me wasn't so bad... it could be so much worse."* The basic answer to that is probably yes, it could be so much worse. But guess what? It's not a competition. Your pain is *your* pain, and all pain is relative and relevant. Do not spend time comparing your hardships to other people's, or beating yourself up because you don't think what you've gone through justifies how you feel today. I promise you, whatever it is, it does. If something affects you, it matters, and your happiness and emotional stability is just as important as the next person's. I urge you to contemplate the following, *"One does not have to be a combat soldier, or visit a refugee camp in Syria, or the Congo to encounter trauma. Trauma happens to us, our friends, our families, and our neighbours"* (Van Der Kolk, 2015). Pay attention to your life and the people in it, and open up your heart to all the difficulties and negative feelings that the past may present you with. Looking back over your shoulder can be tough, but sometimes we must acknowledge that which has gone before us in order to progress to something better.

2

TYPES OF ANGER

As a child, I looked at my father as some sort of superhuman. He was calm, honest and he rarely ever lost his temper. Whenever a line was crossed and he did become angry, it was fleeting and fair, and within ten minutes all was well with the world again. He would tell me he was going for quiet time and I would watch him through the gap between the floor and the bottom of his bedroom door. And there he would sit, in low lighting, on the wooden floor with his legs crossed and his eyes closed, meditating, sometimes for two hours at a time. I was in awe of this practice, of the way he managed to keep so still. His presence created an air that bathed our little flat in calmness and peace. Quite the opposite of what went on at my mother's home. I remember asking him time and again, how did he get to become so smart? So calm? Where did he get all his knowledge? And, most importantly, when could *I* be as smart as him? He used to laugh, not a patronizing laugh but a genuine laugh of total fondness and adoration. He told me that the first step in acquiring any sort of knowledge is admitting that, in the grand scheme of things, you know absolutely nothing at all. The next step, he told me, was to look within. All the tools you will ever need to better yourself and the world around you are already inside of you, he would say.

Before we can even begin to know anything about anything, we first must know ourselves. And love ourselves. Well, here I am twenty odd years later, finally trying to pass on the advice which he *still* gives me to this day, twice a week. We, as people, discuss anger in a very general way. It means this for this person, that for that person, nothing to these people and every-thing to them over there. Your main focus should, however, be on yourself. It's ok to be selfish... After all, it is ourselves we are trying to work on. Here's where things get a little scary—the point at which we must begin to admit to ourselves what we are really like, and no longer rely on the personas we have carefully crafted over the years. I warn you, you may not always be pleased with your results, or very impressed with certain ways you've acted at points in your life. It is true, no matter how timeworn and corny it is, that no one is perfect. It is in judging our behavior and reflecting on ourselves, however, that we begin to move forward and recognize why we are the way we are. And let's be honest, who better than ourselves to do it?

CONNECT FOUR

So, with this in mind, let's take a closer, more personal look at anger. I think we've hammered the point home enough that anger is a sort of umbrella term for many different emotions, but it also has a number of variations within itself. There are different types of anger, and different ways which people choose to respond to them. Taking a closer look at what sort of anger we feel most often, first and foremost, can perhaps give us a more detailed inclination about what's going on beneath the surface. The clock has struck the thirteenth hour of honesty, let's begin! Overall, we can consider anger in four distinct forms when trying to suss which flavour of rage tickles our taste buds most often: "Justifiable Anger," "Annoyance Anger," "Aggressive Anger," and "Temper Tantrums" (Ni, 2019).

Justifiable anger constitutes some sort of principled, righteous outrage. This might be at the sorry state of the world, social and environmental injustices or the way the couple across the street treat their children. It's the type of anger we feel when we are sat in front of the television on a Wednesday night and Cody, the abandoned pup, or Pixie, the overworked donkey, flash up on the screen. That sharp pang of rage mixed with a considerable amount of accountability and guilt that we feel for those people and things that are in horrifying, unjust situations is what we can call justifiable anger. This type of anger is arguably the easiest to transform into something positive. The rage we feel at the dishonesties of our governments, and maltreatment of our fellow humans is what motivates us to answer our call to action. If we can learn to channel this, and harness it into an energy that can be controlled and directed, then we can become activists, encourage change and make a real difference in the world. However, maybe it's time to question why you are so enraged? It is natural, of course, and part of being a good human is that we possess the innate desire to help those in need, but ask yourself, is it becoming too much? Are you obsessing over everything else around you so much that you are forgetting to look within? Does the raw anger you have toward your abusive neighbour stem from anything that is going on in your own life? Or has gone on in the past? It is a useful technique to question every step of every emotional process in your mind, ask yourself why some things trigger you more than others, or why you are more motivated to help out in certain situations than in ones you deem less important. You might surprise yourself.

Next up we have annoyance anger, which is arguably the most common type of anger because it is the one most of us experience on a day-to-day basis and does not necessarily always stem from deep-rooted issues. This sort of anger is also not necessarily full-blown Vesuvius rage, but could be slight frustration or annoyance at the type of things that rub us all the wrong way every day. Is it normal to feel frustrated and annoyed at common things that irk the average human being? Yes. Is it normal to feel enraged and irritated every day? Multiple times a day? Multiple times a day to the point it accounts for the majority of your daily mood? Hmm, not so much. This being said, "normal" is a funny word. After all, what the hell is normal? One man's idea of wacky and weird is another's boring. And certainly, in terms of mental health, everything and nothing is normal at the same time. But we need a bench mark, and if you are starting to feel your frustration growing to almost become a part of you, it might be time to take a step back and re-evaluate what's going on inside. If you're wondering how to tell if your rage levels are approaching unhealthy on the ever-sliding scale, there are some simple things you can consider. Pay attention to how long it lasts—is it a brief irritation that soon settles back into a happy middle? Or do you find yourself simmering on the edge of explosion for several minutes or more? Do you find yourself internalizing trivial problems, or taking things that are almost definitely not directed at you to heart? More often than not, you will find that, not dissimilar to your justifiable anger, you are obsessing over trivial non-issues, which is in turn causing you to stifle and suppress the real issue. If the steam is coming out your ears five minutes after someone has accidentally caused you to drop your purse, it's time to give this its due consideration.

We're heading into uncharted waters now, however, this is often a sacrifice we must make if we want to find our buried treasure. Let's talk about aggressive anger. This is your school bully, malicious lover, abusive parent type of anger, and is one that can do a lot of damage. You may be a victim of this type of aggression, you may *be* this type of aggressor—if you are, it is important to remember you are likely a victim too. See, this type of anger, though it is centred around asserting dominance and control, has firm roots in the soils of insecurity. We all know that it is usually the bully that actually has the most profound and heartbreaking problems in the end. For someone to feel the need to harm, dominate or diminish someone else, means they are not happy within themselves. It is as simple as that. People who harbour aggressive anger, and even those who act on it, are not always bad people. It is highly likely that people with this kind of anger inside them have suffered some sort of trauma or memorable negative experience. The sad fact is that about one third of people who are abused, for example, will later go on to become abusers themselves (Goleman, 1989). People who are exposed to violence or neglect are more likely to blame themselves and feel ashamed and hurt, which we all now know can easily lead to becoming enraged. Unfortunately, many people in this position are not educated about how to cope with anger, or understand that sometimes the hand life deals us doesn't even seem worth playing. It's not your fault, it is just how it is. So, where do you turn to? Alcohol, drugs, violence and crime are all popular stops on the high speed anger train, but it is really important to know that it is *never* too late to get off. Admitting that maybe you have been toxic (trust me, we all are at times), overbearing, insecure, jealous or out of line is not a thing to be ashamed of. Quite the contrary, self-reflection and admission to the fact that we can do better is one of the strongest things a person can do in their lives. I'll say it again, the answers are not to be found through the hole you punched in your drywall last week, they are inside of you.

Last but certainly not least, we have temper tantrums. Yes, it sounds like the type of thing a toddler suffers from when they throw all their toys out the pram because they are not getting their own way. And that is *exactly* what it is. Do not take that the wrong way and think I am insulting you as though you were a child, believe me, temper tantrums and raging outbursts were pretty much a trademark of my personality at one point. That is the point I want to keep reiterating: there is *no* shame in this process. We've all done it, we've all seen red and flew off the handle, causing a tornado in place of what should've been a gentle breeze, you just might struggle with it more than others. These outbursts do, however, usually begin in childhood, and are quite fundamental in how we develop and grow emotionally. If you have attentive, loving and emotionally intelligent people around you to guide you, normally we grow out of this phase after as little as a few months. However, for many of us that is not the case. These unjustified, excessive and unrestrained tantrums are really a cry for help, and a sign that we need to be shown what is appropriate and what is not. Would you blame a neglected child for being confused, perhaps scared and therefore angry? No, or at least I hope not. Well, if we are left with these feelings as children, how can we expect our adult selves to heal on their own? Of course, we can learn as we grow, off of our friends, partners and general social expectations, but if there is something within us that has not been dealt with, some rage that has been left to fester and gather more and more energy, then this is not enough. It seems unfair, but it is the same for every human on earth—sometimes, we have to clean up a mess that wasn't ours to begin with. But it is now. As adults who are seeking to better ourselves, it's time to admit to losing our heads, causing unfair damage and to maybe hurting those around us in the process. Remember, we can grow up at any age, and just because you have more physical years on you now doesn't mean you're not carrying baggage around with you from decades ago.

There is a common thread, a connection, that weaves its way effortlessly through every type of anger that we have just talked about: look within yourself. Anger is an outward expression of an inner problem. Once we can identify what is really going on inside of ourselves, we can control our outward behavior far more easily. Examine your life, your ups and your downs, your friends, your family and even your enemies. All of them, or most of them, have had parts to play in your life and your experiences, the person you are today, reading this book. Struggling with anger is not a sign that you are a bad person, or that you will never "get better," it is a sign that you have an imbalance within, and since when was that something we couldn't control? I urge you to consider the Law of Polarity, found in the Kybalion, a magnificent work by The Three Initiates. It states that *"Everything is Dual; everything has poles; everything has its pair of opposites; like and unlike are the same; opposites are identical in nature, but different in degree; extremes meet..."* Think about that for a second. If all energy is the same, just presented in different degrees, then we can use this when considering our anger. If there is no absolute, then we know that there is another side to our anger, to ourselves, a softer, more honest and innocent side that we are just not in touch with yet. Once we realize this truth, that there is duality in all that we see around us, and in ourselves, we are able to see things from a different perspective, one from which we can start to make positive change.

How Do You Express It?

As previously mentioned, as well as there being different types of anger, there are also different ways in which we express our anger. Again, this information is useful in deciphering what might be going on inside of you to motivate you to react the way you do, and the way we convey and articulate our anger is usually linked to the type of anger we feel. With this in mind, there are generally three main types of anger expression: Passive, Aggressive (or Open) and Assertive. This is directly linked to communication, and the same exact three types are generally associated with how you present yourself and how you interact with others. They are all pretty straightforward in terms of what they mean, but examining each of them in a bit more depth could help you to decide which kind of communicator and aggressor you are, and why that might be. Consider the following and try to decide which suits you best:

1. **The Passive Aggressor.** This is the "silent treatment" style of anger. Though it may not be shown on the surface, it is very much alive and kicking, but most of the time, people who display passive aggression are either fearful or intimidated by the actual idea of confrontation, no matter how angry they may feel. And so, it takes the form of going in huffs, avoiding tasks and people alike, and perhaps the most dangerous of all, bottling things up. Though the whole point of this book is learning about how to manage your emotions, getting things out in the open and engaging in confrontation, when necessary, is actually a healthy part of life and relationships. Those who choose to deal with their aggression passively are almost certainly, and maybe unknowingly, turning up the heat on their pressure cooker of anger and undealt with emotions.

2. **The Open or Aggressive Aggressor.** Ah, one of my oldest and not so much dearest friends. You can probably guess what kind of shape this expression takes. Outrage, screaming, shouting, violence,

bitterness, malice… the list goes on. The word "open," in this case, is not shed in such a positive light as its true meaning. Being openly aggressive means being out of control. Ironically, this type of aggressive expression usually stems from a need to be in control. How paradoxical we human beings can be, huh? It's not difficult to guess the detrimental effects this type of behavior can have on our mental and physical health. The post-tantrum exhaustion, pounding headache from the furious tears and worst of all, the guilt we are racked with at the words or actions we have said or done that have hurt others or ourselves. In short, very little is worth it. Raging, bullying, and controlling will not ever fill that empty hole that we feel in our hearts. Only we can do that. Of course, this is nearly impossible to remember when that hot flash of red strikes us in the moment, believe me, I know. However, acknowledging that our reactions are unhealthy, and questioning *why* we fall so quickly down the rabbit hole of rage is a crucial step in self-reflection. Admitting that yes, I was out of line, I lost my head, I did things I regret, is the beginning of the beginning!

3. **The Assertive Aggressor.** If you have already managed this, or are on your way, more power to you! Though, as stated before, everyone's experience and mode of expression is different, though no better or

worse, this is the most healthy model we can base our expression on. This is healthy confrontation. This is having firm personal boundaries whilst at the same time having respect for the boundaries of others. When you feel that anger rising in your throat, you don't ignore it, but you don't open fire either. You observe it, reflect on it, and take the time to communicate it in a calm and honest way. The two most important aspects of this type of aggression are patience and respect, for yourself and for the others around you. Doesn't sound too much even *like* anger, does it? That's because we get stuck in a place where anger is an enemy, a tool for suppression, and it's really difficult to get out. The good news is, we are never truly stuck if we don't want to be. This might sound like some paradise where everyone talks calmly and doesn't shout or swear or lose control. On the contrary, assertive aggressors can just as easily become enraged as the next person, no one is immune. The idea is to reach a stage where the scales tip, and assertive aggression starts to become the norm. Be patient, as frustrating as that might be...

So, there you have it. Now, these are general definitions, you might take aspects from two or all three, you might match one to a T. The point is, now you're thinking about it. Considering the ways in which we express our anger, and the main motivations we have to become angry, give us some insight into our own mentalities. Take a personality test, look into your birth chart, study yourself the way you would for an exam until you feel like you can't possibly know more. When we do this and take the time to know ourselves, we are finally, you guessed it, looking within. The journey begins.

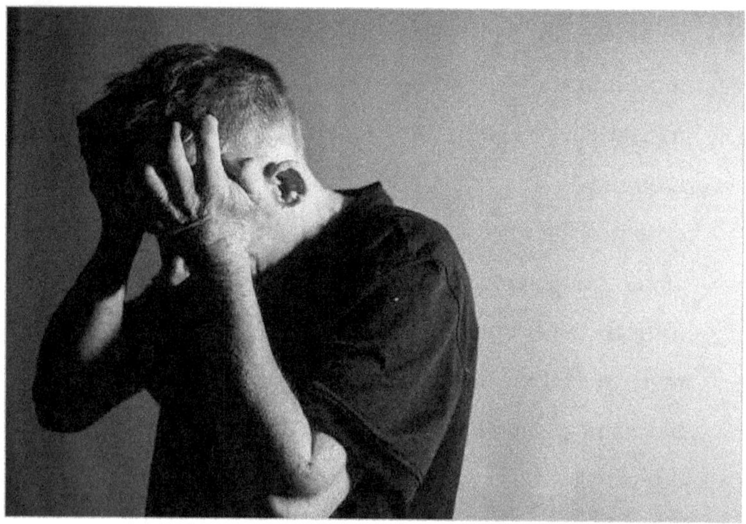

3

A MANY FACED COIN

And so, here we stand, at the foot of the mountain, unsure and somewhat unprepared for the potentially life-changing journey we are about to take. We have but our willpower as our boots, our uncertainty as our compass, our consciousness as our food and water, and our souls as our guides. On this journey, however, we take with us a mantra: *"Holding onto anger is like drinking poison and expecting the other person to die"* (Buddha). It is imperative that we hold onto this during our assent, because it would be foolish and naive to expect that it will be easy, or that we will perhaps even sometimes forget why we decided to attempt it. Think of your path to emotional growth just like climbing a mountain. At times, you will run into obstacles—rocky roads, cruel weather, and, as to be expected, the very real possibility of getting lost along the way. Think of the ground you stand on as your anger, as it is now, raw and real in the bare light of day. The higher you climb, the further away from you it falls until you can see it from a clear distance, not as something that you rely on or need, but as something that you can move away from and revisit whenever you want. That long, winding, never-ending road becomes a mere speck when you have reached a higher plane and attain the distance you need to see it for what it really is. It's a funny thing, perspective, and sometimes it's the only thing we need. So don't be afraid, or rather, be afraid, but embark on the voyage anyway. It is a known fact of life that the things we value the most never seem to come easily, that's why they are worth the struggle. Oddly enough, the Bible springs to mind here, a book I have visited many times in life despite the fact I am more inclined toward spirituality than any sort of religion. Religion is a broad subject, all different kinds, all different beliefs and moral views, and some people choose to not bother with it at all. However, like everything in life, we can take from it that which we choose.

No one is asking you to adopt some new set of beliefs or commit yourself to some sort of order, but the following sentiment is one that rings true to all of humanity, regardless of your beliefs or moral or religious stance:

"Enter ye in at the strait gate: for wide is the gate, and broad is the way, that leadeth to destruction, and many there be which go in thereat: Because strait is the gate, and narrow is the way, which leadeth unto life, and few there be that find it"

— MATTHEW 7: 13-14

In other words, it would be easy to put this book down, ignore our problems and leave the mountain for another day. It would be easy to stay on the path we've always known, the one that seems most familiar to us, despite the negative effects it is having on our lives. It is not uncommon to begin to suffer from Stockholm Syndrome with our emotions—our anger becomes the kidnapper or the abuser that we keep running back to because, at the end of the day, it's the only way we know how to be. There is better out there, through the mist and the rain, at the peak of that mountain. Take the risk, choose the road that looks daunting and difficult, because at the end of it, the only question you will ask yourself is why you didn't do it sooner.

A CONSEQUENTIAL EMOTION

Along the journey to emotional growth, we may run into some obstacles. First and foremost, we are concentrating on our anger, yes, however, as previously mentioned, anger interacts with many different feelings—sometimes, anger is how we feel *in response* to another issue. Common emotions associated with anger are fear, anxiety and/or stress and guilt. It is important to acknowledge these also in the regard that while we may become angry in response to these, it is also very possible that anger will *follow or accompany* them. And here we are reminded that anger is usually a sign of deeper problems. Time to explore these in more detail, as these are perhaps the obstacles you may pass and need to overcome on your climb to growth. You are encouraged now, to think of your anger as a phantom menace—a mysterious figure that hides in the corners of your life until, when it creeps up on you, consumes your whole body and mind. You are aware of it, you know that it is there, but it has always been and gone too quick before you get a proper look at its face. This time, you are going to stop it dead in its tracks. Bring it close to you, not as the dark, hooded stranger that takes you by surprise, but as a familiar acquaintance. What mask is it wearing today? Is the face of this figure still hidden? Sit with it a while, and if you *really* think about it, the mask will soon dissolve into nothing, and what lies beneath will be revealed.

First, let us examine fear. Fear and anger actually stir up lots of similar symptoms and feelings, though they are not the same emotion. For example, when you are scared, it is natural for you to feel that sudden loss of appetite, rush of adrenaline and increased heart rate. This is usually the sort of feelings we experience when we find ourselves in a situation in which we go into "fight or flight" mode. In this section, I would like to cover two distinct but not dissimilar types of fear that may be associated with anger. The first is immediate fear, where we are suddenly in some form of danger or find that there is an oncoming threat or imminent danger to our health and well-being, or that of someone else. As aforementioned, though we have evolved to become the intricate beings we are, we still possess that indigenous, instinctual will to survive. You've probably heard the phrase "the best form of defense is attack," and while the truth in this is somewhat unclear and open to debate, it is how many of us react when we find ourselves in trouble. Though this sounds like an instance where you find yourself lost and alone in the middle of the woods standing two feet tall against a grizzly brown bear, this immediate sense of fear is felt throughout the world, every-day, in seemingly normal situations. Examples of this are work-place or school bullying, and abusive relationships, be it physical, emotional or sexual, be it between friends, partners or family. Hell, fear is half the reason discrimination exists. Fear of minorities, religious and ethnic groups, different genders and sexualities lead to anger and hatred against these groups, and for what reason? Normally simply because we don't understand them, we are afraid of the unknown and so we lash out in order to protect ourselves from it. It's a tale as old as time though it's still a very common pattern of human behavior...

Why do you think politicians use it so much? Each day, people are placed in situations that force them into "fight or flight," and when we think we are faced with a threat, sometimes we get angry. This can be a good thing, and a good mode of survival when we're in real danger. However, if you think back to the chemistry of anger, it is the amygdala, the emotional centre of the brain, which activates this sense of fear and distress. Remember what happens if the ever-logical cortex doesn't catch it in time? The left side of the brain practically shuts down and we react completely based on our emotions. Sometimes we may genuinely be in danger, sometimes we're not, but react as though we were. This could be a perceived personal attack, something as little as taking something said tongue-in-cheek the wrong way. If we already struggle with emotional dysregulation, we are especially likely to have unjustifiable reactions to overall "safe" situations. This is where the explosions commence, or where they begin to simmer. When we perceive the people around us as constant threats, always waiting for the next time we have to jump to our own defense, we are not focused on what's going on inside of us, or paying any attention to the damage we are doing to our emotional well-being. Call me geeky, but George Lucas (the writer of Star Wars) hit the nail right on the head with this one: *Fear is the path to the dark side. Fear leads to anger. Anger leads to hate. Hate leads to suffering"* (Yoda). When we are afraid, we often feel the need to stabilize, or "cancel out" our fear with anger. We feel scared and out of control, "weak," and we think that we can regain some control or appear "strong" if we express anger. In the end, both create an energy of irrefutable negativity. We cannot replace one negative emotion with another, we must learn to face that which makes us feel it in the first place.

This leads me to the second type of fear, which intertwines a lot with shame and guilt. This type of fear might be the product of something that initially sent you into fight or flight. This type of fear is secondary, the remnants of ash that fill your lungs from that initial bomb of terror. This is trauma. Though we will explore the ins and outs of what trauma actually means later on in this book, it is important to acknowledge it as an issue that really *must* be addressed if you are finding yourself held fast in the jaws of anger. When we are traumatized, we are haunted by experiences, triggers and memories from the past. This can take many shapes—a few of the most common are abuse, neglect and/or early exposure to things such as addiction, sex, violence, and even bereavement or heartbreak. Post-traumatic stress disorder (PTSD) is a very common mental health issue that many people suffer from who have experienced trauma. Emotions such as fear, shame and guilt are intricately inter-twined with this sort of mindset. Am I to blame for the break-up of my parents? Did I mean less to my father than the booze? Could I have done something more to stop her from doing it?

Or simply, *why* did it happen? And, scariest of all, will it happen again? These are often questions that haunt a fearful and traumatized mind that has not yet properly processed and dealt with incidents from the past. When you are scared, confused and guilty, do you really want to face those feelings? Nope. So what do we do? We get angry. We unleash these painful feelings of hurt in the form of aggression, frequently losing control and doing nothing but adding to the fear and shame. Or, if you're a passive aggressor, you hold it in and let it fester, grow and transform into an even bigger ball of fury. Considering the possibility that we are so angry because, underneath, we are still scared children who were never able to deal with trauma alone, and understanding that we still have a chance to face our fears can be crucial—before we become so lost that our fear turns into fear of ourselves. I leave you with this:

"Fear keeps us focused on the past or worried about the future. If we can acknowledge our fear, we can realize that right now we are okay. Right now, today, we are still alive, and our bodies are working marvelously. Our eyes can still see the beautiful sky. Our ears can still hear the voices of our loved ones"

— THICH NHAT HANH

Angry Anxiety

Ever since I was a child, whenever a situation made me feel anxious or stressed out, I used to pick my eyebrows out, one by one, until there was nothing left above my eyes. Every time I did it, my mum would shout at me and tell me how ridiculous it looked. I would go to school wearing fake glasses to hide the patchy spots where my eyebrows should have been. And I become furious at the world. In hindsight, I was furious because I felt so misunderstood, by my mum, by my friends, by everyone. I became bitter, spiteful and got to the stage where I was almost asking for situations to become stressful, just so that I could pluck out my eyebrows. It hurt, too, but I didn't care. You end up so lost in the stress and the rage of it all that you begin to detach from yourself, and you no longer even care enough to try and fix the damage. I was an angry teenager, as many are, but my point is that it is easy to get into a cycle of thinking you are coping when you're not, at any age. I coped with my anxiety by obsessively plucking hairs out of my face, you might try to balance your stress by using anger. For the record, I ended up angry anyway—replacing one thing for another is not how we achieve growth or solve the problem.

Anxiety is a major player in the anger game. Though not always the case, anxiety is also a symptom of past trauma, and holds a firm position next to fear, shame and guilt in these situations. Some of you may be reading this, however, and don't feel afraid, ashamed or guilty, except for that which maybe your anger has caused. Maybe you're wondering if this is the path for you, or that you're *just fine* compared to some others. Trauma and fear are not the only faces of this coin. Anxiety, stress and every-day frustrations that begin to build are just as justifiable reasons to end up becoming angry. Are you feeling constantly stressed about your actions, appearance or outward persona? Are you liable to conjure up devastating scenarios out of very little before the future has even taken place? Do you feel anxious in social situations? Well, past research has, in fact, shown that "personal perfection, anxious overconcern, blame proneness, and catastrophizing (are) predictors of general anger" (Zwemer, 1984). Isn't *that* interesting?

Anger doesn't always have to stem from some suppressed childhood memories or life-altering events. Sometimes, you're just a bit stressed out. Sometimes this is in our genetic make-up, in other words we are anxious by nature, and sometimes this anxiety is caused by external factors, everything from trauma to an important presentation at work. Regardless, the effect it can have on your mood and emotional wellbeing remains the same. Anxiety can lead to anger for a number of reasons. If you have ever had an anxiety attack, or a panic attack or something similar, you know how horrible it is. You can't even keep up with your own heartbeat, you hyperventilate and struggle for air, your thoughts race in circles around your head and you break into cold sweats all over your body as it trembles. It can sometimes take up to an hour or more for these attacks to settle down. I knew a girl who ended up seeking anger management therapy because she was just so damn sick and tired of having panic attacks. The very fact she *had* them sent her into blind rages. And I didn't blame her. Feeling anxious over standard and routine situations can become a thankless task—endless worry and confusion, a high-speed mind 24/7 and often no real understanding of why we feel this way. This, as I will continue to emphasise, is the problem, and the point at which your anxiety and stress can turn to anger. We *must* know ourselves in order to articulate and process what we are going through. If we are constantly on edge, we will become resentful and frustrated very quickly—come on, we're only human. This irritation with ourselves and with the world is the gentle push that puts us on the slippery slope to becoming angry. Add that to the mix of nights of stress-filled insomnia, keeping up relationships with family and friends, plus academic or workplace worries, and you have a very bitter tasting recipe. And so, we lash out, snap at the wrong people and prioritise the wrong things. You might have previously thought that an important deadline at work and being neglected as a child have nothing in common... look again. Granted, these scenarios are different in manifestation, but the feelings they evoke are the exact same, perhaps just varying in degree. They are both situations in which we feel an unrest within and a lack of emotional balance and overall well-being, and they are both situations where we often choose to cope by turning to anger. The key, as has been said so many times before, is to identify the true cause of why you're angry, and therefore frustrated, and therefore anxious. Grab it by its roots and you take the power back, grab it by its roots and you can start living your life on your terms, and not on the terms of the past. The next time you flip a coin, think of your anger and its faces. Think of its clever disguise, how it cloaks your fear, your guilt, your stress in a mysterious rage. When it hits the ground, picture your anger freezing in its tracks, and as you cover it with your foot, remember that, no matter what side it has landed on, you are in control. So... Heads or tails?

4

LET'S TALK ABOUT TRAUMA

Ok, so we have established in the previous chapter that anger has many faces, and is often attached to feelings like fear and shame. Various reasons for these emotions were also talked about, one of them was trauma. But what really *is* trauma? How does trauma relate to anger? Why is there going to be nearly a full chapter dedicated to trauma alone? The answer is as big as the question. Our trauma changes who we are as people, it dictates how we form relationships with other people, how we process the every-day, how we act and react and, most notably here, how we process our emotions. Yep, trauma is a big one, and it doesn't come alone. Trauma is also linked to a vast number of mental health disorders that are deeply associated with anger. This includes things like PTSD, Emotional Dysregulation, and Borderline Personality Disorder, all of which will be discussed in further detail.

First, picture this. Are you ever walking down the street, or having some lunch with friends, or quite simply minding your own business when all of a sudden you freeze? Perhaps a certain song has just come on the radio, or someone has just walked past you wearing a certain perfume, perhaps someone calls you by a certain pet name or touches your shoulder in a certain way. Maybe you've been startled by a loud noise, or feel a sudden gust of wind. Whatever it is, you are instantly transported back to a time and a place from which you're longing to escape. When those triggers are pulled, you, the bullet, fly through the years, months, days or however long, until you are stuck fast in mid-air, and forced to relive those moments you're running from. This happens to us when we are traumatized. Notice the range of instances that might stir up these not-so-old emotions. The list goes on and on, because triggers are as vast as that which they trigger. There are any number of different reasons a person might suffer trauma. There are the big ones, yes, such as sexual assault, physical or emotional abuse and death, but that's not all there is to it. Traumatic events also include things like road or plane accidents, natural disasters, living through war and terrorism, break-ups and losing, or even nearly losing, loved ones. Basically, any event that has occurred in your life and has damaged you emotionally, whether you've been neglected or humiliated, rejected or hurt, trauma can happen at any age and to anyone. Like anger, it does not discriminate. Never think that what you have gone through does not merit feeling traumatized or triggered, and similarly, never feel that you have gone through too much to ever find your way back. The road might seem dark and unclear, but it is always there, even if uphill. Dealing with trauma can be painful, and can include some painful re-reads of books you wish you'd burned long ago. Remember that re-reading gives you the opportunity to re-write. Though it may seem like you are taking steps backwards, or re-opening cold cases to no avail, you are always progressing on your journey to growth. Often, we need to look back in order to understand where we are and where we're going.

WHAT'S THIS GOT TO DO WITH ANGER?

Human beings are survivors. We source food and water, we seek shelter and we protect our young and ourselves from harm as best we can. We spend our lives manning our defenses that are constantly under construction with each new experience that we learn from. The fact is, there will be times where we, or someone close to us, come under attack. Anger, being that it is actually a basic key aspect of survival, is often how we respond to this. It focuses our energy into overcoming a situation in which we might crumble and surrender to otherwise. When we are experiencing a traumatic event, often one of the main objectives is simply to survive. So we switch to offense, and channel our energy into just simply getting through it. This is fine, actually, it's great and necessary at the time. Channelling our aggression and our need to endure and prevail can sometimes be the difference between life and death, but what happens when we can't get out of this mindset? If, when we are triggered, we are thrust back in time to the traumatic event in question, then we must also start to feel the same emotions and have the same thoughts that we did at that time.

We remember, we relive, and we get angry. The question is no longer "fight or flight?"—we cannot run away, and we cannot fight the situation because it is already over, instead we become frozen. When we are frozen in a constant state of trauma and anger, it is difficult to sustain leading a normal life. Anger is often our response when we feel we have been mistreated, or treated unfairly. If we have suffered unexplained loss or tragedy, or have been hurt or neglected without valid reason, we might get angry. Anger and betrayal go hand in hand, whether this is betrayal from a friend, a partner, family, or the universe in general. Usually, if we are traumatized, we have gone through some form of perceived wrongdoing to ourselves or our loved ones. There is often little or no explanation, or whatever explanation remains cannot explain away the pain of what has happened. Your triggers, your unquenchable thirst for answers, and the hurt you feel about what you've gone through are all things that set your course on what I will call the hamster wheel of trauma. Your mind is constantly hyperactive, you struggle to keep your head above water, and, in simultaneous efforts to escape the past and embrace the future, you find yourself unable to go anywhere. We end up reacting to every-day situations as though they are traumatic, with the same anger and stress-levels that we would feel if we felt our lives were in danger. This is especially common in war veterans who have returned from combat. After months, or perhaps years, of death, explosions, and loss, something as simple as a car backfiring might send a returned soldier into a panicked frenzy. This is the cycle that repeats no matter the situation. The brokenhearted girl doesn't trust the perfectly nice guy no matter how perfectly nice he is because of the scars an old flame has left behind. The neglected son is inexplicably angry at any kind of authority because he was abandoned by those who should've guided him to the right path. The young woman is terrified of intimacy no matter how desperately she wishes to truly experience it because of the warped manner in which she was exposed to it by her stepfather. The old man on the bench can't use public transport anymore because he lost his wife when a train derailed forty years ago. The situations differ, the effects of trauma don't. Look inside yourself, examine your past and try to pinpoint the times when you felt traumatized, there may be many times this has happened. Compare how you felt then to how you react to things now. Any similarities? As painful as it may be, could taking the time to visit these moments in our lives actually help us, in the end, to let them go? The answer is yes. But remember, take your time. As we've discussed before, these things take time, and rushing to the finish line means not really doing the job properly.

So how does anger manifest itself in the face of trauma? Over the past century, there have been invaluable developments in the exploration of the brain and how it processes our emotions and experiences. In the past, someone might have walked into the office of a psychiatrist and would have walked right back out into a mental institution and labelled a crazy person. From there, some patients probably suffered more, from gruelling and literally mind-numbing treatments such as electric shock therapy. This, of course, was wrong and uninformed. Nowadays, thank goodness, things are much different. Scientists, psychologists and doctors alike have put their heads together to come up with some answers to the extensive question of how the human mind works. In relation to trauma, there is one diagnosis that comes up again and again: PTSD (post-traumatic stress disorder). Research has stated that general anger, overall bitterness and antagonism are closely linked to PTSD (Galovski et al., 2014). Before going any further, it is really important to note that words such as "disorder," "issue" and "problem" often appear when talking about mental health and trauma. Do not take this literally. There is no problem or issue with emotional imbalance or having to do some work on yourself. Literally nobody on the planet is perfect, and everyone goes through ups and downs at some points in their lives. There is no shame in this, and even if at some point we are diagnosed, as many of us have been, this is actually a positive thing. Finally, thanks to modern medicine and psychology, we have some answers. We can pinpoint how experiences meander through our brains, what they leave behind and why. We can uncover tracks that had previously been totally snowed under and, in turn, start the process of healing. How do we characterize PTSD? Who can suffer from it? Like trauma, and anger, anyone anywhere can suffer from PTSD—it is the result of undealt with and lingering trauma. When we experience a traumatic event and become distressed, our fight or flight activates, the emotional side of our brain goes crazy whilst all logic flies out the window. In other words, we don't process things in a natural, rational way. So when we go back to deal with it, we find that we can't.

Minute details, such as certain tastes and smells related to the experience become unbearable and we are unable to move forward. Instead, we might suffer from insomnia, flashbacks and invasive, unwanted memories that plague our minds. This is what PTSD is, living in, and suffering from, the past, we are unable to put the trauma behind us and it can even begin to interfere with our daily lives. Think of it as unwashed dishes. You're doing the housework, but you can't bring yourself to do those dishes, they are too dirty and overwhelming. Each night, you tell yourself you'll deal with it tomorrow until even the thought of it is keeping you up at night. It pops into your head at random points in the day and starts to cause you anxiety and irritation. And, as ever, the longer you leave it, the worse it gets. The process is the same with PTSD. You cannot face the trauma and so you leave it and let it fester—though you're not dealing with it, do not be under the illusion that it's going away. Anger has actually been said to be one of the "hyperarousal symptoms" of PTSD (Tull, 2020). The reasoning for this is somewhat obvious. When we experience trauma, we are frozen in a state of danger and threat. Afterwards, we may no longer feel in control of our emotions or even our lives, we may feel under constant attack and like the world is no longer a secure place for us to be. Anger is our response to this. It is our way of coping with threats and the thing that motivates us to strive for survival. Like we said in the beginning, this is good and often life-saving when we need it, but to constantly live in that state is to live a life unfulfilled. Treatments to such things will be discussed in the following chapters, but for now:

"Experience follows intention...all we need to do is recognize our thoughts, feelings and perceptions as something natural...we simply acknowledge the experience and let it pass. If we keep this up, we'll eventually find ourselves becoming able to manage situations we once found painful, scary or sad...We'll realize that we're always sheltered, always safe, and always home"

— YONGEY MINGYUR, RINPOCHE &
SWANSON, 2009

Other Possibilities

Though extremely common, PTSD is not the only mental health issue associated with anger. On the contrary, there is a vast array of mental conditions that are closely linked to anger. It might be worth your time, if what you're about to read sounds familiar, to do some digging into whether or not you may be affected. Please do not let this dismay you if it is indeed the case, use it as a platform to start from. There are medical and spiritual treatments out there that really can help you contain your emotions and pave the way to emotional growth no matter how helpless the situation may feel. A particular mental health issue associated with anger is IED (Intermittent Explosive Disorder), where individuals suffer from impulsive temper tantrums and volatile rage. This disorder does not necessarily need to be caused by the environment—like Border-line Personality Disorder (BPD) and Emotional Dysregulation (ED), it can be inherited genetically, or simply can stem from the make-up of your particular brain chemistry. All of these can, however, stem from trauma. With IED, it is particularly likely that the person in question has been exposed to violence or lived in an explosive household from a young age.

If you lose your cool on the regular at seemingly small issues, speak with your fists and harm yourself or others, you might want to take a look at this. People with IED are controlled by their rage rather than *being* in control, and this, if left untreated, can lead to serious damaging consequences. BPD is also closely associated with anger. This disorder is often caused by a range of factors, including things like neglect, abuse, exposure to alcohol and drug abuse and even things like a lack of serotonin in our brains. People with BPD often struggle to form stable, meaningful relationships, have warped perceptions of themselves and of others around them, and suffer from serious emotional instability, such as never-ending fear and, of course, anger. Often, people with BPD will have a pattern of self-loathing and self-destruction, as well as feelings others will be out to get them. This leads to impulsive behavior which, if you spend your time feeling angry and scared, can be really detrimental.

This takes us back to our need to survive—we use our anger to motivate us to endure situations, but in the case of BPD, if we have suffered from neglect or the feeling of rejection, our anger can also turn toward ourselves. This is a big issue as that is where self-harm and/or substance abuse might come into play. Then we have Emotional Dysregulation (ED). ED has long been acknowledged as a fundamental symptom of mental health issues surrounding trauma, though it also stands alone as an issue (van Dijke et al., 2013). People with ED struggle to regulate their emotions, particularly their fear, sadness or anger. Again, people with ED find it difficult to form and sustain relationships, or process their feelings in a "normal" way. We all feel angry, scared and sad sometimes, but people with ED feel inexplicable and unstoppable fury, terror that freezes their soul and devastation that might make their heart physically hurt. I should know. This also leads to substance abuse—it is, after all, the "quick fix" to the problem, the "fad diet" when trying to lose weight. It offers temporary relief to the harsh reality of sobriety, but in the end, doesn't treat any of our emotions. We still end up angry and bitter at the world.

We are all but children. The way we are today, and so many of the mannerisms and behaviors we have learned come from how we were treated as children, or the environment we grew up in. If we are never shown the correct path, how are we expected to find it? If we have been left to pick up the pieces of traumatizing events, direct or indirect, without the help we need, how can we expect ourselves to not feel broken? Our anger can manifest itself in any of the ways we have discussed, our job is to find its birthplace. There will be no shame here, only answers, truth and growth. You may be guilty of subconsciously attaching a stigma to mental disorders as so many of us do, but if you look inside yourself and ask yourself, in the mirror in the cold light of day, what really matters? The answer is you, your happiness, your stability and your inner peace. You just need to be willing to do anything to achieve it.

5

VICIOUS CYCLES, BROKEN RECORDS

"Fall down seven times, stand up eight"

— JAPANESE PROVERB

By this point, you are probably getting a bit out of breath. We've discussed, at length, what anger is, why it plagues us, where it comes from, how we deal with it and so on. By this point, you have possibly and quite probably forced yourself to think about some potentially painful and distressing times in your life. Maybe even reading this has made you angry. That's okay. Be angry, feel how you feel and keep on going anyway. You've now come too far on this hike to turn back and miss out on the spectacular views from the top. As you progress, you will slowly begin to feel your strength returning to you and the curve will flatten until you feel like you're walking on air. The beauty of this process is that it doesn't end when you reach the top. There is nothing in this life that can be learned absolutely. There is always room to grow, knowledge to acquire, and more peace to be obtained. It is the gift that keeps on giving.

So now that you're here, with lots of hardship behind you and still a steep road ahead, you've reached a turning point. This is the point at which we discover the point, the point at which we commit ourselves to breaking the cycle and promising to do better by ourselves and our loved ones. Feel the angry, hurt, rejected, humiliated part of your soul that's desperate to escape and let it breathe, let it go. Do not be ashamed of it, do not interact with it or act upon it. Stand very still and let yourself feel, but don't do anything about it. In doing this simple task, we have just proved to ourselves that our emotions do not need to dictate the way we live our lives. We have just shown ourselves that we are in control of our physical bodies despite how we feel, and, with the right tools and exercises, we will soon learn how to work toward more positive mindsets. It would be so easy to just turn back and reduce ourselves to our previous states. At least we understand ourselves then, right? But, really, do we? Or have we just become so accustomed to feeling negative and angry that we'd rather stick to the status quo than take on the risk and the challenge of breaking free? Is the past just too unbearable, or the act of asking for help just too shameful? It is quite the paradox. Why, when we feel so angry and upset, would we *rather* do nothing about it? Pitch your tent and rest for the night. Reflect on how far you've come so far and consider the importance of carrying on once you realize why this record has been spinning for so long:

"It does not matter how slowly you go, as long as you do not stop"

— CONFUCIUS

WHY AM I STUCK?

It is all too easy to find yourself stuck in a rut. You know you're unhappy, you can almost feel the lows coming before you hit, you might even try to say, "Ok, today I am going to make an effort to stay calm and rational," but you find yourself falling into the same patterns and routines. This probably has a lot to do with the fact that anger, in itself, is a cycle. There are different stages of it and each one leads logically and effortlessly onto the next. You have to ease yourself out of your anger—it is not unlike addiction. We become addicted to being victims, addicted to avoidance and addicted to the illusion that becoming angry and violent means we have regained some form of control over our lives. It doesn't. However, understanding things like the cycle of anger and the cycle of trauma allows us to pinpoint the exact stages in the process at which we are losing control, and more importantly, why. Once we do this, we give ourselves a side door, a different perspective on our anger which allows us the opportunity to break the vicious cycle.

The cycle of anger, in its physical terms, is this: A triggering event occurs which spurs on negative thoughts. These negative thoughts then evoke emotional responses which cause us to feel distressed, irritated and angry. We then start to experience the physical symptoms of anger, such as racing heart rates, sweating, dizziness and tremors. This becomes overwhelming and then we react, and finally give a communicative response to these feelings. This is when we lash out, by screaming, shouting, or whatever preferred form of outburst you have. When written out on paper, it actually seems quite rational, how anyone would react in this situation. The problem is, when we are triggered, we normally don't have the time, the logical judgment, or the concentration to stop and observe the stages of our emotions as they are happening. However, this is what we are trying to learn, and is actually highly achievable if we put our minds to it. There is another phase in this cycle however, that is one of, if not the most important reasons that explain why we keep going back. After we have calmed down and the storm has passed for now, we start to realize our words, our actions and our behavior and we start to assess the damage we have done. And, always right on time, the guilt, regret and self-loathing enter the room. Lots of us will feel low, depressed or even numb at this point. It is during this time that we convince ourselves that we do not deserve help. We do not deserve to get better or feel better or indeed receive better because we are lost causes. We might even never properly calm down and still feel too angry at the world and the injustices that have been thrown upon us to even stop to think about feeling better.

The longer you leave the anger and the negativity unprocessed, the more difficult it is to find the motivation to break the cycle. The same way the longer you leave your dishes, the more they pile up. Another thing we humans do that doesn't help the situation, is that we catastrophize the thought of taking action before we've even attempted to. You skip class so many times that you can't even face *the thought* of going back. You leave your room untidy for so long that the mere *idea* of cleaning it up makes you anxious. But then you go back, you start to tidy, and you realize "hey, this isn't as bad as I thought it was going to be."

Dealing with our emotional instability is no different. Of course someone neglected in childhood will never feel good enough, or a bully victim will be wary of new people they meet. We often try to compensate for this by becoming angry and aggressive, and become so wrapped up in trying to feel some sort of control that we become stuck. We then spend our time either beating ourselves up for getting angry in the first place, distracting ourselves from the dreaded thought of doing anything about it, or frozen in past mindsets of traumatic events. We convince ourselves of imminent danger and attack, we tell ourselves people are out to get us, we take things personally that have left the other person's mind seconds after the fact. And all the while we are exhausting ourselves by going round and round in circles.

No matter what you've been through, where you come from or what you've done, you deserve to feel better. No matter what loss or grievance you have suffered, or watched someone else suffer, you are entitled to feel angry and in pain. You matter, you are important and so are each and every one of your experiences and feelings. Once we start believing this, we are already thinking about things more carefully. We must repeat the cycle of anger like our buddhist mantra until we can actually visualize its stages and react in real time with a cooler head. It all comes back to understanding ourselves and pinpointing where these angry emotions come from. We must do this for ourselves, first and foremost, but also for those we love and care about. These aggressive cycles can continue for years and be passed down through generations. Why, when we have the opportunity to break them, would we choose to breed negativity? The cycle of anger and how we get stuck in it is completely logical, but nowhere near as logical as the reasons to break it!

Your Emotions Don't Define You

Many of us would make the argument that we act, react and interact in a particular way because of our emotions. How many times have you equally heard and said the phrase "well I can't help how I feel"? I have some news for you, you absolutely can. See, our emotions—how we feel about things—definitely influence our behavior and the choices we make. But, essentially, we are responsible for our own behaviors and choices.

It would perhaps appear at first as a classic example of what came first? The chicken or the egg? Our emotions or our perceptions? Well, research shows that actually to begin your journey on the road to a more positive mindset and way of thinking, the first thing we must do is look at how we perceive the world around us (Edelstein & David Ramsay Steele, 1997). This would suggest that, in actual fact, it is our perceptions that come first.

We have emotional responses to external factors based on our expectations of the people we meet and the situations we find ourselves in. You'll have heard about the dangers of assumption, or the naivety of having too many preconceptions of things, yet we just can't help but continue to do it. We build up a core set of beliefs about life, people, relationships and experiences, and this is what all of our reactions are based on. You'll have noticed that although you may have felt like your whole world has come crashing down, you're in too much pain to carry on and surely life must come to a stop, it never does. You continue to live and breathe, the sun continues to rise and fall, and life goes on. Then, in some time, you wonder why you were ever so upset. This is because our emotions do not define us. Think of yourself not as an angry person, but as someone who, right now, is feeling angry. It is important to note that, although our emotions do not define who we actually are, they must not be ignored. Putting them in their place is not the same as suppressing them and leaving them to simmer and boil over. We simply have to uncover why we perceive the world the way we do—going over the trauma in your life is a good starting point, as is simply from the beginning.

So much of who we are and what we learn stems from our childhood, it has a massive part to play in the belief system that we then apply to the rest of the world. We must find the flaws or distortions in our thinking and aim to reform the way we see the world. Think about it, if our emotions and external situations controlled us, then surely everyone would react to circumstances the same way. The reason everyone reacts differently to things is simply because they have different perceptions of the world, and therefore, different emotional reactions. It's why some people grieve for months over an ex-lover, and some have moved on within a few weeks. In the end, no matter who you are, if we deal with our emotions healthily, they eventually fade into nothing and until our next experience. So carry on. As you sit on the hillside and watch the clouds passing you by, liken them to your experiences. Acknowledge them, give them a name and let yourself feel them. But remember that they will not last forever, and the one true person that can change them is you—that is why you should get up and continue this journey.

6

MANAGING ANGER

It's time for some good news. We've talked about the fact that we are not confined in any way by our feelings and experiences, and that the ball is always in our court to get up and do something about it. This is much easier said than done, and you will have days where you feel angry, sad, affected, and everything else and that is completely okay. As you already know and always knew deep down, there is no quick fix and patience is key. I know that saying "be patient" to someone who struggles with anger issues is undoubtedly the last thing anyone wants to hear but hey, it's the truth, and that's what you picked up this book for. The amazing thing is, the second you decided that something should be done about your temper, your trauma, your personal issues and/or whatever else is making you so angry, you already paved the first bit of your path to growth—it is potentially the hardest part of the whole process. This is one of those things, like addiction or heartbreak or grief, that cannot be resolved unless you really want it to be and have the courage to admit that you need some help. Plus the fact that, first and foremost, you have to do it for yourself. This is not to say that others can't help you, support you and even influence your decisions, but the path to growth—spiritual, emotional or psychological—is one we ultimately must take alone. This is because everyone is different. Your path may meet someone else's, or head in the same direction for some time, but it will never truly stay this way. Though this may seem a lonely thought at first, there is also no one to preconceive, to expect things from or to project onto. Just you and the road. At this point, you have taken the time to get to know your anger, to understand where it comes from, how it manifests itself, and perhaps most importantly, to recognize that it is not actually a fundamental part of your being and is something that can be managed. You have been fully equipped with the information and the tools to start building your new and improved view of the world and yourself. It's time to learn how to use them. So where the hell do we start?

CONTROLLING THE UNCONTROLLABLE

What we mean by "anger management," is really to establish, utilize and dispose of our anger in a healthy way. There are loads of different ways in which we can achieve this. One of the questions you will need to ask yourself is whether you want to take on this task yourself at home (which is totally fine and down to personal preference), or whether you are open to leaning on the support of professionals. Basically, do you want to go to therapy or not? And this really does depend on the individual. I would argue, now, that everyone in the world should give therapy a try at some point in their lives.

Before, however, my view was entirely different. I remember thinking, "Why *on earth* would I want to go and talk to a complete stranger about any of my problems when I can barely handle them myself?" To me, it was spending money I didn't have and time that wasn't worth wasting on fixing something that apparently did not need fixed. How wrong this assumption was. I'm not ashamed to admit I sat in silence for the first three weeks, so much anger with so little answers and a teenage chip on my shoulder because the world was obviously out to get me. I cringe to think back now, but it's a natural part of growing up. No more natural than admitting we maybe need a bit of help. But this truly is really difficult. It's not just about the fact that we can barely come to terms with things in our own heads never mind trying to articulate them to a total stranger, but if we are already angry and have a warped perception of those around us, how can we feel safe? If the fear of getting judged, or having our secrets spilled, being humiliated or perhaps rejected has consumed us our whole lives, then the idea of therapy might be a little more than daunting.

However, and this is a fact, none of these things will happen. First and foremost, therapists have a lawful duty to keep what you share with them confidential, and it is their literal job not to judge you. However, it's more than this. As I started to feel more and more comfortable, and edged closer to opening up, I decided to just ask the questions I had been pondering in my head for weeks: *Do you not get bored? Do you never want to tell anyone what people tell you? Is it not difficult to not judge people? Or think badly of them?* Consider the answers. She urged me to change my thinking, and before questioning what could go wrong, to ask myself, "What would motivate someone to be a therapist?" The answer is quite simple: 1. The desire to help people, and 2. The desire to understand people. Why, if someone wants to help you, would they judge you or make you feel unsafe? Why, if someone wants to understand you, would they tire of you or let your trauma affect their opinion of you? It doesn't make sense when you think about it like that. It may be the case, however, that therapy just isn't for you. After we discuss its benefits we will talk about loads of other alternatives we can do at home. I would only encourage you to not make the decision until you have at least tried it. What do you really have to lose?

So, with this in mind, let's talk about therapy. There is a vast array of therapy types, and sometimes, before we even begin, we have to spend some time digging for the right kind of therapy for us. We are focusing on our anger, but remember if there are other issues that need addressing, there are other options that might suit you better. We're going to discuss Counselling (talk therapy), Psychotherapy and CBT (Cognitive Behavioral Therapy) in relation to how we can learn to deal with our anger issues. Counselling is a form of talk therapy, which, as you can imagine, encourages us to talk about our problems. Counselling sessions are usually somewhere between 50 minutes and two hours, though this is dependent on your needs. So is the amount of time you might wish to see a counsellor—this could be from four weeks to four years. There isn't a time stamp on how long you will want to use counselling, however, it is probably the most general form of therapy for anger issues. Whilst it is fantastic to be able to sit and voice your feelings and concerns out loud, and whilst counselling can offer things like coping techniques and positive mental advice, often we need something a little more specific that is perhaps more tailored to our kind of issue.

The great thing about basic counselling is that many schools and workplaces offer it for free—it is treated as a part of the curriculum in schools and as part of the workforce across various different jobs, which should be further proof to you that help is normal and help is your friend. Delving deeper into the world of therapy, we arrive at psychotherapy. In counselling, you can use your therapist as a sound board, and the main focus is on discussing your feelings and emotions and explaining how they are impacting your life. Psychotherapy seeks to travel further back into your past. You, the gift, spend time unwrapping your many layers until what lies beneath is finally revealed.

While psychotherapy offers all the upsides that basic counselling does, it is a more intense, more distinct and more precise evaluation of why your mind works the way it works. Though this might seem scarier than the idea of going and having a chat and a rant, it is more likely to establish *why* you feel how you feel and *where* it comes from—in other words, it teaches you to look within and discover the actual root of your problem... sound familiar?

When it comes to anger management, it seems that one of the most effective forms of therapy is actually a branch of psychotherapy called Cognitive Behavioral Therapy (CBT). CBT is so popular and effective because it has an end-goal and an overall aim. CBT not only seeks to help people identify the underlying cause of their anger, but also to actually help an individual to reshape and rectify previous harmful thought processes and belief systems. The one thing that CBT does not always consider in detail, is the past. It is much more of a "here and now" type of psychotherapy which concentrates on the "today" of your emotions and your actions. This being said, if it's necessary to make meaningful progress, of course the past may be examined. However, CBT might, for example, be the type of therapy you seek out once you have already identified what issues in your past have caused you these negative emotions—the main focus of CBT is getting better *now*. CBT operates based on two main elements, the cognitive side and the behavioral side. Cognition refers to our thoughts and feelings, the version of ourselves that lives inside our brains and takes the brunt of our emotional hardships. Behavior refers to our actions, how we interact with others and our emotions, and the ways that our behavior affects these other areas of our lives. The two aspects do not always carry equal weight, and you may need to work harder on your emotions or your behavior depending on what sort of issue you are experiencing. For anger, however, both are extremely important.

So how does it work? Well, first of all you will try to address, with the help of your therapist, where your issues stem from (why you might be so angry). This is normally a relatively short process and is more designed to get the ball rolling, so to speak. There are then three main features of CBT which you'll normally explore with your therapist. These are your Automatic Thoughts, Thinking Errors and Strategies that can help you cope with them (Muris et al., 2008). Our automatic thoughts are the assumptions we make before a situation has even played out. These are based off of the preconceptions we have formed about the world and include things like assuming people are out to get you, or you're always in imminent danger. And so we have our distorted thinking—the way we view the world around us and the type of expectations we set for ourselves and for others. This might include things like catastrophizing or internalizing and personalizing everything (blaming yourself).

The strategies we learn in CBT are the tools we will use to try and combat our warped perceptions and intrusive negative thoughts. This might include things like relaxation techniques or role playing out situations in order to try and change our way of thinking. So there you have it, a quick guide to what your therapy might entail should you choose to give it a try. With CBT, the one thing to consider is how much it focuses on the present. If you are really struggling with past trauma that requires more detailed attention, it might be an idea to try another type of psychotherapy first, like trauma therapy. It is important to note that it will probably not be easy, and whatever type of therapy you choose, will require some work on your part. You must force yourself to be patient and open, as difficult things in life do not just fix themselves overnight. Expect difficulties, expect tears and expect frustration—the likelihood is you will be talking often about triggering situations or memories and, at times, it will feel like a struggle. However, we couldn't have the rainbow without the rain, and the good news is that there is no rush. You can window shop your way to the therapist that feels right for you.

Hopefully, those of you that would have rather died than sat yourself in that hot seat in front of a total stranger to talk about the deepest and darkest corners of your life have changed your minds, or are at least slightly more open to taking the chance. For those of you who still don't want to face it, not to worry. For one, therapy can be somewhat self-taught—there are numerous books and articles about techniques to calm your mind. Also, the very aim of therapy is that you don't need to attend forever. With types of psychotherapy like CBT, the actual aim is to equip you with the tools you need to manage and sustain your emotions and your behavior on your own anyway. It can be difficult and even mundane at times, but I promise it's worth it.

Managing Anger at Home

Of course, while therapy can be really beneficial and change our lives for the better, ideally we would like to be able to keep up the benefits of it on our own. This means going home at night and knowing that we have the mental willpower and capacity to control our emotions all by ourselves. Whilst some people like to climb the ladder rung by rung in the care of a professional, others might feel more comfortable teaching themselves. This is totally fine, but in the long run, will require just as much effort, courage and patience as going to therapy would. As we have talked about before, the main priority is identifying where your anger might come from and sourcing a tangible starting point which we can retrace our steps in life to better understand where we are today. Once we have done this, the goal is to face our issues and try to deal with them head-on, rather than suppressing them and channeling them via our anger. There are a number of ways you can do this. Talking is a good start. No problem if you don't want to go to therapy! Talk to your friends, your family, your partner or even yourself. Write a journal and keep a log of triggers that cause you to feel anger, go back and study them as though you will be examined on them and try to suss out the common factors that lead you to become angry.

Once we have a good grasp on what triggers us and why, we can start to deal with the emotions in real time. Of course, you will not become a prince or princess of Zen overnight, but as you move forward and keep track of your progress, eventually it will become second nature. The main thing to keep in mind is that it is really useful and important to have a routine. However, we must ensure that it is not too rigid and that we don't become obsessive over it. This is because life happens too fast and things change every day. We don't want a situation where we replace our anger with a routine so intense that it might actually become a trigger if interrupted. And it will be at some point, such is the nature of life. Consider things like exercise, sleeping and eating times, what you're eating, who you're spending time with and how much time you are spending with yourself. One of the great laws of the universe is that balance is the most important thing in our lives, within and without. How can we expect to be balanced within if our lives are coming at us full pelt and out of control all the time? Admittedly, the idea of every human being walking around dedicating the correct portion of time to every aspects of their lives and themselves sounds like some sort of paradise Utopia and admittedly, yes, it is extremely difficult sometimes to fit in our mental health when we have kids, work and all of life's other curve balls. However, it is not unachievable. You must figure out what makes you happy and go for it. Sleep for eight hours a night, eat three good meals a day at decent times and spend time in nature. See people that make you feel good and don't forget to snatch some seconds away for self-reflection and a good book a few times a week. Once we put the aspects of our lives in the correct position, everything else starts to fall into place. There will be days when we simply don't have the time or the energy, and life will come at us too fast and we will sleep for four hours, live off of a banana and six coffees, and be too tired to even think about our mental states by the time our heads hit the pillow at night. That's okay. Just don't lose sight of what is important, and what's important is you. You worry so much about how things in your life will turn out that you forget that it depends, most of the time, solely on you. Always try to see situations from another side, just so you at least know that there *is* another side. Remember, your anger is not who you are. Most importantly, don't forget that it's never too late to ask for some help if you need it, you can even download and access online courses that can advise you on various anger management coping techniques. You are never alone.

7

PEACE OF MIND

The quest for inner peace is something that, in my experience, is considerably overlooked and brushed past for a lot of people despite how important it actually is for our quality of life. It's all well and good to say "get into a routine," "do what makes you happy," "prioritize the important things," but how do we do this? With anger especially, it is often nearly impossible to even know what the important things are because we are constantly wound up so tightly. Doing the aforementioned, and forming good habits and thought patterns is absolutely what we should be doing, but we need to have at least partial peace of mind to be able to do this. We need to be aware of the now and be present in the moment, we need to come to terms with letting go of that which we can't control, and we need to exercise both sides of our brain when we encounter situations so that we can always see it in a balanced light. This is impossible if we don't take any time for ourselves to slow down, just as we discussed in the beginning.

Working on yourself means carving out the time to dedicate to doing so, and being willing to persevere if things get tough or don't change as quickly as you might have hoped. Emotional growth is a core aspect of living a happy and healthy life. It needs to be nurtured and cared for the same way all the other parts of us need to be, but it is often one of the most overlooked parts because we "don't have the time." Because once we are in the habit of not dealing with our emotions, or worse, when we lie to ourselves so much that we start to believe we actually have, it becomes too easy to ignore our issues and take the easy road. The journey you embarked on to establish an inner equilibrium and learn how to control your feelings was never designed to be easy, and this is what makes it so worth your while.

So, what is it we are actually trying to achieve here? Well, when we are sad, we try to do things that will cheer us up, when we are scared, we try to find things that will bring us comfort and security, and, when we are angry, we want to calm down. Notice that a sense of calm is the common thread that weaves through all of these different scenarios. In short, that is what we are trying to achieve: a sense of calm. More importantly, we want to get there naturally. The goal is not to swap emotions for distractions, to bury ourselves in work, the gym, or our substance of choice. Instead, it is to reach a sense of peace and balance within ourselves purely on our own, so that we have the *right mindset* to enjoy all of these things in a healthy way. There are an endless number of books on this subject, some even centuries old, and some of which are much of the inspiration for the book you are reading now. The answers are there if you wish to find them, as they have always been. Often we look, but we don't really see what's in front of us. We acknowledge problems, but not enough to do anything about them. One sure-fire way to change your mindset, open your eyes and propel you toward calmness is meditation. Personally, I feel that things like meditation should actually be taught from the moment we are enrolled in education as children. It's almost a guarantee that it will stand you in better stead than learning how to balance simultaneous equations for three hours a day but hey, I don't make the rules. Still, it's never too late to learn. Every day is definitely a school day, and the school of life is always where we will learn the most.

MEDITATION VS MINDFULNESS

Right now, you're probably picturing a Zen monk with a shaved head, draped in simple robes, sitting cross-legged and perfectly balanced on a mountain top at sundown. His eyes are closed, his breathing is deep and pure, and the whole earth seems to quiver as the sacred chant of his "Om" ripples throughout the atmosphere. This, believe it or not, can be achieved in the comfort of your own bedroom. The practice of meditation itself dates back thousands and thousands of years, as early as the 1st century, with particular strongholds in India, Japan and even ancient Greece. Over the centuries, ancient teachings, books passed on through generations, and scribbles on the walls of people sat in meditative worship, have accumulated into how we know meditation today. It is deeply connected to religion, and is practiced widely throughout Hinduism, Christianity, Judaism, Buddhism and Islam. This being said, meditation is not strictly religious, and can be practiced from a secular point of view as well. Rather than being about religion, it is more about spirituality. It is used as a way to connect with our higher self and bring our thoughts and feelings within their speed limits so that we can slow down and examine them with more care.

In turn, we are able to separate those thoughts we want to invest in from those that are causing us harm or bad feelings. It also teaches us how to relax and how to breathe properly, in a way such that we can let go of the anger or hurt that has led us to sit down and cross our legs in the first place. Meditation was brought to the West by Paramahansa Yogananda, an Indian monk and yogi, who made the journey from India to America, and brought with him some of the best-kept secrets of achieving inner peace. This is, after all, the whole point. To be "Zen" is to feel content and tranquil with our thoughts and feelings, and realize how insignificant yet invaluable we are to the world around us. It is about accepting our place within the greater universe and having the self-awareness that enables us to consider life both subjectively and objectively. Research also suggests that meditation actually has physical health benefits as well as mental ones. Studies have actually shown that practicing meditation can slow our heart rate down and even bring down our blood pressure. As well as this, it can dramatically reduce our anxiety and increase our quality of sleep (Davis, 2006). Seems like a pretty good package deal if we are struggling with anger, right?

Speaking of package deals, you will probably find that it is quite common to see the words meditation and mindfulness in close proximity of one another. Though it is true that they often come hand in hand, they are not the same thing. Meditation is a practice, something we set aside time in our days for. When we meditate, we try to clear our mind of distraction or any outward thoughts by doing things like focusing on our breathing or repeating a mantra. Mindfulness, on the other hand, is the practice of completely focusing on the here and now, on the present moment, free of judgment and past or future worries and concerns. We can do this at any time of the day, in whatever situation we are in and in the presence of whoever we are with. In other words, "mindfulness is the awareness of some-thing, while meditation is the awareness of no-thing" (Shapiro, 2017). The two concepts complement each other, and one can be nurtured and elevated by the other. Like meditation, mindfulness and paying attention to our thoughts, feelings and behaviors as they occur, can improve our focus, alleviate stress and spur on our emotional and spiritual growth and intelligence. If we are able to, in this case, concentrate on and observe our anger and even our physical reactions to it without distraction, we can begin to understand how to control and even prevent it. Ideally, we want to reach a stage where mindfulness and meditation become a part of our daily routine. First of all, you need to work out what will work best for you. There are different types of meditation, six popular ones in particular. Normally, you'd need to look into each one and decide which suits your needs best. Lucky for you, this next part will tell you, in brief, what you need to know to best make your decision.

1. **Mindfulness Meditation.** This is probably the most common form of meditation in the Western world, and is arguably the best for dealing with anger. As you've just read, mindfulness is the practice of focusing on the present moment, without judging anything that's going on. The aim is to try and separate yourself from your thoughts and emotions—rather than becoming subjective and therefore opinionated, observe and contemplate them as they pass you by. Creating this gap makes you perceptive, you have the freedom to choose which thoughts to engage with and which ones you're better off ignoring. This is also your best bet if you don't have someone to guide your meditation.

2. **Focused Meditation.** This may be good if control is an issue for you. If you feel you have little or maybe even no control of your life or feelings, this meditation

is good for focus and self-discipline. To avoid distraction and bring our focus to be solely on the meditation itself, we can turn to our senses. If focusing on your breathing doesn't work, try leaning on exterior influences. This could be listening to a calming but consistent sound or staring at the flicker of a candle. This form of meditation trains our brains to force themselves into a state of presence and of calm, and therefore is particularly nourishing and affirming when we feel like we are not in control.

3. **Movement Meditation.** If you are the restless type of soul and find that your body and mind works most effectively when in action, then this is the meditation for you. Yoga is the most popular form of movement meditation, however you can do this by simply going for a gentle stroll, or any other form of movement in which you do not exert yourself too much. Your mind must still be able to focus on the task at hand.

4. **Spiritual Meditation.** This is when we seek to connect and engage more profoundly with our creator or god. This type of meditation is more likened to being in a state of prayer, and encourages us to open our hearts to creation and all that is in it. If we have suffered from trauma in the form of neglect or even bereavement, this type of meditation can bring us a sense of comfort and an ease to the longing for love that we feel. We remember, when engaging

in spiritual meditation, that we are never without love.

5. **Mantra Meditation.** This is when we use a phrase or series of words or sounds to empty our mind of distraction and judgment. Repeating a mantra gives our minds something to focus on when they find themselves drifting back into the chaos that is our every-day thoughts. If, for you, silence is deafening, then this is a good one to try. It keeps your mind active and still creating an element of sound whilst simultaneously making you more susceptive to your environment and everything in it.

6. **Transcendental Meditation.** If you are committed, willing and *ready* to make meditation a prominent part of your life, then this is probably for you. This form of meditation is more personal, bespoke even, if you will. You construct mantras and structures that are specifically tailored to your needs and to what you want to focus on. It is slightly more intense than the others just because it is much more coordinated and controlled.

Each form has its own benefits and whatever you choose to do, if you dedicate your time to it, it will work. Also, you don't need to stick with any form just because it is the first one you've chosen. Like therapy, it depends on the individual. It's whatever works for you, and you'll get there. Eventually.

The "How To?"

Once you've decided what suits you best, you need to understand where to begin. The most important thing that you need to do when starting meditation is to keep consistency. You must ensure that you set aside time for it every day, because regularity is what will make it become a natural part of your life and daily routine. The good news is, you don't need to dedicate *that* much time to it, especially if you are a beginner. Ten to twenty minutes is even enough at the start as your mind begins to acclimatize. However, in the time that you do choose, make sure that nothing will interrupt you or distort your focus. You should endeavour to meditate for the same ten minutes every day or night, and it's also a good idea to do it in a space which is used solely for the purpose of meditating. It won't be easy to find your inner peace next to the fridge, the TV or your work computer. Far too many distractions. Your posture is also important. Make sure that you sit in a position that's upright but comfortable, and try as hard as you can to do this without using any back support. Most people prefer to meditate with their eyes closed, and it usually does work better because there is less to look at that can distract you. Closing your eyes brings your focus further inward.

Next, we have to find something to keep up focused. Our thoughts, as important as they are, are distractions from the now. As odd as it may sound, thinking of nothing at all is how we can decipher which thoughts are actually worth our time. This can be achieved by doing any of the things discussed previously such as using a mantra or focusing on the rhythm of our breathing. This all sounds pretty easy. It's not. It is harder than you might think to empty your mind, and you shouldn't be surprised if, for a while, you're finding it really difficult. Some days you might find yourself totally unable to focus. The best thing to do in these cases is to accept it and leave it for a day. As long as you go back and try again tomorrow. Find the balance between not forcing it, but also persevering. Slowly but surely, you will start to feel the positive effects of it. I am reminded of an old Zen saying that I used to have to read ten times a day just to keep up my willpower:

"You should sit in meditation for twenty minutes a day, unless you're too busy; then you should sit for an hour."

So you see, you can introduce relaxation techniques to manage your emotions from the comfort of your own home. Buy a yoga mat, invest in some books, fill your air with essential oils like frankincense and myrrh, and you become that Zen monk that you envisioned on the mountain top. Practicing these techniques will not only help in the moment, but will actually reduce your overall negative emotions all the time. Another technique you could try is relaxing your muscles, one by one, until your whole body is calm. We can do this by acknowledging our respective muscle groups for up to thirty seconds, from our toes all the way up through our legs, torso, neck and head until our entire corpse has been bathed in reflection and consideration. This is a fantastic way of calming down an angry mind. Anger is one of the things that meditation actually works best for as it allows us to contact our higher self, the version of our self that is outside of our emotions and understands that, in the end, we are in control. If our higher self knows this and can practice it, then so does our lower. After all, as above, so below.

8

GOODBYE, ANGER

Perhaps this is where you were expecting to read something like, "Ah, and so we reach the end of the road," or "that's us finally at the top." Alas, this is not the case. Unfortunately, you cannot expect to reach the heights of emotional growth and soothe your long-term anger in eight small chapters. It is likely that you are still at the very beginning of your journey, and it is important to know that this is okay. You may not have reached your mountain peak, but you are well on your way. This may be a flurry of pages bound together by those same eight small chapters, but (hopefully) it has given you a new sense of motivation, drive and desire to confront your emotions.

When we say goodbye to our anger, we are not saying farewell in the sense that it will all of a sudden be rid from our bloodstream, but we are saying farewell to the way we once knew it.

It is no longer to be looked at as an enemy, a menace, or an overpowering stranger. Instead, we look at it now as a guest in our house, just as was discussed in the beginning. We welcome it in, acknowledge its presence, and know how to tell it when it is time to leave. We say goodbye to the confusion, the lack of control and the shame, and embrace instead reflection, compassion and understanding for ourselves. Remember, from the Kybalion, that everything has poles? Here, we exercise this law. All ends eventually meet and transform into their supposed opposite. This is what we have done with our anger, and in doing so, we ourselves have become forces to be reckoned with. When we manage this brave act of changing our perception of our anger, we can actually start to see the potential within it.

Of course, it's not a pleasant emotion, it can stem from really unpleasant memories and/or experiences, the consequences of it are often harmful, and it usually leaves us feeling negative or low. All these things aside, anger can be used for good. If we learn how to channel it properly and direct it at the appropriate causes in a healthy way, it can even become our friend. Always remember, anger is an emotion. Anger, in itself, is not actually what causes the harm or the damage, though most of us would rather blame our behavior on it just to avoid facing the real root. It's like the saying "guns don't kill people; people do." Whether you agree with this or not, there is validity to be taken from it here. A loaded gun is, after all, an inanimate object that can cause no harm to man nor beast unless someone pulls the trigger. This can be useful when we think about our anger. It takes courage, discipline and honesty with yourself to be able to acknowledge the fact that, angry or not, we are in control of the decisions we make. We decide whether we are going to pull the trigger and who we are going to direct the gun at every single time. Yes, our emotions can influence our reactions and sometimes it might even feel like they are the ones responsible. However, in the end, the onus is always on us, and it takes guts to be able to admit this. Note that once you do, you will see things in a totally different light again. When we stop lying to ourselves, stop wallowing in the idea that we are victims and take some responsibility, we are not so quick to lose control. Everyone behaves differently when they can be held accountable, and everyone *must* hold themselves accountable in order to grow. Okay, tough love lesson over. Now we can talk about how we can use our anger for good, and why it is so important that we do so.

ANGER AS OUR FRIEND

Anger, as much as it gets a bad rep, one of the positives we can take from it is that, by its very nature of being an emotion, it communicates with us in relation to our character—it can actually give us valuable information about ourselves (Matthews, 2019). So, when you feel angry, rather than focusing on the negativity of the emotion itself, ask yourself what it is trying to tell you. Remember that anger, when put in its place, is a healthy and valid emotion, and that sometimes you will absolutely have the right to be angry. The trick is learning the difference between when your anger is justifiable and when your anger is irrational.

As we discussed in the previous chapter, meditation is a good way to figure this out. However, justifiable or irrational, it would be preferable that no real damage to ourselves or to others is done. It all comes back to looking within. If we can tune in to what our anger is trying to tell us, we can recognize the benefits of feeling this way, and look at it more of a hazard warning of an underlying problem, rather than an excuse to trash our bedrooms. So, with this in mind, consider the possibilities of using our anger for good. First of all, anger can be a clear way to draw up boundaries. It is really important in life that we assert ourselves and our needs, and that we do not settle for anything less than fulfillment (within the realms of reality). For example, if you are in a bad relationship, or a friend isn't treating you right, that feeling of anger alerts you to the fact that something is not right and you are potentially being mistreated. The key is to recognize this before we fly off the handle and do more damage. You have a right to be angry and to express your emotions and let the person know you are unhappy, you do not have the right to become violent or harmful. It's a fine line that makes a huge difference once crossed. Another thing anger is good for is motivation. This could be in any sense, maybe you're angry at some injustice in the world or maybe you're competing against someone in a race or for a job promotion. This type of anger is great for getting us the hell out of bed and forcing us to grab the task at hand by the reigns. The extra adrenaline and want for control often really pushes people to do the absolute best they can do. Again, you have the right to feel angry and to channel this into your work ethic or philanthropic drive, you do not have the right to use it *against* other people who are undeserving of it.

As we've talked about before, anger also gives us the courage to tackle challenges that are presented to us. This may be something fairly trivial to something of grave seriousness, and anger is usually the tool we use to propel ourselves into action. It can even save our lives. Finally, we can use our anger to indicate that we are earnest, genuine and deserve to be heard. Whether it is proving our dedication or devotion to something or someone, or whether it is expressing dislike for how someone has treated us, or how we have seen someone else be treated, it is a way of saying, "look, I'm serious." In the end, anger actually can be seen as a sign of strength, but it's the when, the how and the why that people get confused with.

Anger is a sign of strength when we can control it and articulate it in a way that gets our needs and problems across without damaging the feelings (or the property, for that matter) of ourselves and others. Smashing up a door frame, for example, is not. Belittling or patronizing someone to feel better about yourself is not. Being vindictive, malicious and vengeful is not. We all have the right to become angry sometimes. Remember that if it wasn't meant to be felt, then it wouldn't exist. Our emotions are our guide to how things are going in our lives, they tell us lots about how we perceive the world, and the things that trigger us teach us why we might think this way and where it comes from. Anger, like all the others, is a tool in the exact same way. Admittedly, because of the intense physical response anger causes (the blind rage and all that), it is much harder to catch in time before it spins out of control. Do this just once, however, and you will know you can. Listen to your mind and your body, take notes on what your reactions tell you about yourself and begin to address the real issue. Once you do this in any given situation, you'll begin to find that your original fury has dwindled considerably, as you have received the message that you are trying to tell yourself. Think of it like your emails. You have your inbox, spam, sent and anger folders. As the mail flutters in in the overwhelming way that most emails do, slow down and take the time to read them. You'll find that, in the end, you'll have a better understanding of yourself, and the desktop of your mind will feel much clearer.

Spirituality and the Laws of the Universe

On a last note, it's important to take a look at how our emotions interact with our souls. Emotional growth walks hand in hand with spiritual growth, and it is in, you guessed it, finding a balance, that both can be achieved. Whether you are a believer in this type of thing or not, there are important lessons that can be learned by paying attention to what the universe is telling us. First of all, let's properly define them both and distinguish them from one another. When we talk about spiritual growth, we are referencing our quest for meaning, and our desire to connect in a truer and more profound way with the world around us. It is achieved when we start to act and react based on our morals and what we believe to be right—in other words, when we stop becoming hypocrites and start living under our own judgment. Emotional wellbeing is how content we are within ourselves and the various aspects of our lives. This is when we can start putting our thoughts in their place and examining our emotions both subjectively and objectively so that our judgment and reasoning is always balanced. They each compliment the other —as we grow spiritually, it is likely that our emotional wellness and intelligence will be enhanced and vice versa. Anger and spirituality might seem like a clashing pair at first, but there is lots to be learned from this partnership.

It is important to note that anger and aggression are not the same thing. Anger is merely a feeling, the same as happiness or sadness, whereas aggression is the *way we behave in response* to feeling angry. The two are often tarred with the same brush, hence why many think of anger as anti-spiritual. On the contrary, what if someone is angry at the oppression of others? At the disregard for something holy? At warfare and violence?

Anger, in actual fact, can be both empathetic and even humanitarian. It is, as ever, how we choose to deal with it that determines whether it is good or bad. So, there is actually a spiritual aspect to anger, and we can use means of spirituality, like meditation and mindfulness, contemplation and reflection, to begin to heal our anger. Think of them not as opposites but as forces we can join together to create a positive outcome. Once we shift our perception, that which once seemed to be a hindrance or an obstacle becomes a tool to become better. Living by our principles and searching for a deeper meaning in life ultimately makes us think more about our actions and what's really important. This, in turn, feeds into our journey to emotional growth and helps us to slow down and start to see things for what they are. Before you know it, your anger has actually become your informant, your guide in some situations, and even your friend. Improving your spiritual and emotional intelligence are the two main keys that will open the doors to enlightenment. If you commit yourself to the challenge, chances are you will find yourself happier than you have ever been before.

There is one last law that you should look at before this book draws to a close: the Law of Rhythm. We discussed the Law of Polarity in previous chapters, and similarly, the Law of Rhythm teaches us about the nature of life, the universe and of our emotions. It is also located within the Kybalion. It states:

"Everything flows, out and in; everything has its tides; all things rise and fall; the pendulum-swing manifests in everything; the measure of the swing to the right is the measure of the swing to the left; rhythm compensates."

What this means is that everything, humanity, animals, nations, nature, *everything* is always in constant motion. No living thing is fixed in any one way, and this constant flow is the nature of our lives. The image of the pendulum is used here to try to show us what this motion looks like: we feel happy, we feel sad, we get sick, we get better, we win, we lose, we live, and we die. The "pendulum," so to speak, is in perpetual movement. This is an innate truth of life and this is why it resonates so profoundly. It is both comforting and daunting simultaneously. It is comforting in the sense that it assures us that when we are feeling bad, even on the brink of giving up, the tide will rise in our favor again and things will feel better.

All things will come to an end, yet the process of change is never-ending. This is where it understandably becomes a bit daunting—in realizing this law, we accept that we cannot control the winds of change, and they will continue to blow whether we like it or not. This is great when we are feeling low, but not so great when we realize that the good things change too. However, this is all a part of what we are trying to achieve —the sense of inner calm and peace to accept, and to let go. In the end, when we stop trying to control that which is out of our control, and accept that the nature of our emotions and of the greater universe is ever-changing, we find peace. The trick is to find the point at which you feel most calm and neutral. When you establish what gives you this feeling, of being grounded, hold onto it. Then, when that pendulum swings, it swings with less intensity. Your life and your energy are still ever-changing, and you may not have control over this, but what you do have control over is how much it will affect you and what you do about it.

You might feel angry now, but you will find calm again, you might feel frustrated and hurt, but, one day, you will find peace. That day depends entirely on how badly you want it to arrive. You now know everything you need to know to guide you. You will find beauty you never thought possible in the simple act of letting go.

CONCLUSION

This time, she tells me the news and it hits my ears with a dull memory of the sound it made before. A twinge in my arm, a sharp intake of breath, and is that slight increase in my heart rate? The beads of sweat are still forming on my forehead and palms, but I remain in silence. I do this because, for the first time, I'm paying attention to the look on her face, the nervous uncertainty in her eyes. *Think before you speak, think before you speak.* My inward mantra, though simple, has become highly effective. I say it firmly in my head until the ringing in my ears is drowned out. In through the nose and out through the mouth, I attempt to inhale the reality deep into my lungs, and exhale my distorted perception into the atmosphere, where it disintegrates. A few minutes have passed now, and nothing is broken. The air has not been shattered with obscenities, the doors remain open and un-slammed and I find myself, sitting next to her, eyes closed, quietly crying. This is the first time I have talked myself down, in real time, without help or prior knowledge. Suddenly, I've forgotten what she's told me and am instead aware of the things I need to tell *her*. First of all, I'm sorry. Second of all, I'm not happy with this, or this, or that. She's not happy with that either, okay, so we'll do this. Great. An hour and a couple of cups of coffee later, I feel calm, more weightless than any outburst ever made me feel. So this is what it's like to handle your emotions! I can't lie, it's hardly enjoyable, and takes a lot of willpower and *a lot* of forced compassion. But it works. And one day, I didn't say my mantra, I didn't have to force myself to see the other side. I just did. Is it always that easy? Absolutely not. Have I lost control of my emotions since then? Absolutely. You'll trip up over your choices and fall into the pits of consequence, what's important is that you make the choice to get back up and keep running. It is by making this choice that all the others will fall into place.

LETTING GO

There is no such thing as life after anger. You will never suddenly feel yourself detoxed of all negative emotions or immune to irrational reactions. That's just not how it works, especially when it is something that you might have struggled with in the past. This may sound extreme, but it is not unlike coming off a drug. When we are addicted, we don't think about who we are hurting or the consequences of our actions. Our minds are not clear enough or capable of questioning why we feel the way we feel or how to start addressing it. Both are mental conditions that always have a cause that is normally overlooked and forgotten until we are so caught up in ourselves that nothing else begins to matter. You know what else they have in common? The very first step to healing is admission. Recognizing that we are in a bad place and need some help getting into a better one is by far the bravest thing you will ever do. It is so easy to indulge your ego, or think things like, *"well I'm functioning just fine,"* or, *"I don't need help,"* or even worse, *"I don't deserve help."* We all say these things to ourselves and let our pride, dignity and underlying shame get in the way of what's really important. Let it go. Just let it go. You should look in the mirror and you should like what you see. You shouldn't hide your beautiful soul beneath simmering trauma, irrational guilt and tainted ways of thinking.

You and everyone else deserve so much better than that. Your friends, family and loved ones also deserve the best version of you that you can give. Your work and your hobbies and passions deserve the most dedicated attention you can give them. It all starts with letting go of that voice in your head that tells you things are fine the way they are when your gut knows that they are not. It might not ever truly disappear, the way our anger never truly goes away, but you can learn to mute it. The same way you will learn that your anger doesn't go away because it's not really the source of your problems. Once you figure that out and begin to deal with what is, anger will take its place at the harmonious dinner table and you'll realize you don't even mind having it around.

The Path We Leave Behind

It is imperative that you remember that the state of affairs you trail behind will be what someone else happens upon. We create patterns and waves with the choices we make and the way we choose to act. We gravitate toward people, and them to us, based on how we live our lives and how we allow others to perceive us. A piece of advice that has stuck with me through years of therapy and months of, often frustrating, meditation sessions is this: Whatever you do, wherever you are, try to leave the world a better place than it was when you got here. This doesn't mean you should try and change the course of history, or do some great and noble act that will save humanity, though I'm rooting for you should you choose to. It means the here and the now of your world, the worlds of those around you and whom you care about. It can be selfish and selfless at the same time. Look after yourself, nourish your own needs and share your light with others in your life. You have no idea the people you'll meet and the places you'll go. How can you spend your time cultivating a happier, more loving world when you're so angry all the time? The answer is simple, you can't. So be open, be patient and above all, be kind to yourself. Consider the consequences of your thoughts, feelings and actions, and consider everyone else's too. We all have a responsibility in this life to strive to be good, and to take care of the people and planet around us. Understand that the spark that ignites a lifetime of growth and improvement appears when we decide to take care of ourselves. The difficult thing is, this is only possible when we stop blaming other things. Yes, our feelings and behaviors are affected by things we've had to go through and endure, but at the end of the day, the person we become after the fact is our choice. So choose wisely, nothing is beyond your reach.

"The soul is dyed the color of its thoughts. Think only on those things that are in line with your principles and can bear the light of day. The content of your character is your choice. Day by day, what you do is who you become. Your integrity is your destiny - it is the light that guides your way"

— HERACLITUS

REFERENCES

Bertone, H. J. (2017, June 9). Which Type of Meditation Is Right for Me? Healthline; Healthline Media. https://www.healthline.com/health/mental-health/types-of-meditation

Brantley, J. (2016). Calming your angry mind: how mindfulness and compassion can free you from anger and bring peace to your life. Strawberry Hills, Nsw] Readhowyouwant.

Brewin, C. R., Andrews, B., & Rose, S. (2003). https://psycnet.apa.org/record/2000-13847-008. Psycnet.Apa.Org. https://psycnet.apa.org/record/2000-13847-008

Davis, J. L. (2006, March 1). Meditation Balances the Body's Systems. WebMD. https://www.webmd.com/balance/features/transcendental-meditation#1

Edelstein, M. R., & David Ramsay Steele. (1997). Three minute therapy: change your thinking, change your life. Glenbridge Pub.

Galovski, T. E., Elwood, L. S., Blain, L. M., & Resick, P. A. (2014). Changes in Anger in Relationship to Responsivity to PTSD Treatment. Psychological Trauma: Theory, Research, Practice and Policy, 6(1), 56–64. https://doi.org/10.1037/a0031364

Gardner, D. L., O'Leary, K. M., Cowdry, R. W., & Leibenluft, E. (1991). https://psycnet.apa.org/record/1991-21460-001. Psycnet.Apa.Org. https://psycnet.apa.org/record/1991-21460-001

Goleman, D. (1989, January 24). Sad Legacy Of Abuse: The Search For Remedies. The New York Times. https://www.nytimes.com/1989/01/24/science/sad-legacy-of-abuse-the-search-for-remedies.html

Grohol, J. M. (2018, July 8). We Are Responsible for Our Own Feelings. World of Psychology. https://psychcentral.com/blog/we-are-responsible-for-our-own-feelings/

Matthews, A. (2019, February 2). My Friend, Anger. Psychology Today. https://www.psychologytoday.com/gb/blog/traversing-the-inner-terrain/201902/my-friend-anger

Muris, P., Mayer, B., den Adel, M., Roos, T., & van Wamelen, J. (2008). Predictors of Change Following Cognitive-Behavioral Treatment of Children with Anxiety Problems: A Preliminary

Investigation on Negative Automatic Thoughts and Anxiety Control. Child Psychiatry and Human Development, 40(1), 139–151. https://doi.org/10.1007/s10578-008-0116-7

Ni, P. (2019). 4 Types of Anger and Their Destructive Impact. Psychology Today. https://www.psychologytoday.com/us/blog/communication-success/201905/4-types-anger-and-their-destructive-impact

Potter-Efron, R. T. (2007). Rage: a step-by-step guide to overcoming explosive anger. New Harbinger Publications.

Shapiro, E. and D. (2017, May 23). The Difference Between Mindfulness and Meditation. Medium. https://medium.com/thrive-global/mindfulness-meditation-whats-the-difference-852f5ef7ec1a#:~:text=Where%20mindfulness%20can%20be%20applied

Smith, J. (1998). Breath sweeps mind: a first guide to meditation practice. Riverhead Books.

Star Wars: The Phantom Menace (Episode I), 1999.

Tolle, E. (2004). The power of NOW: a guide to spiritual enlightenment. Namaste Pub.; Novato, Calif.

Tull, M. (2020, February 10). How People With PTSD Can Express Anger Constructively.Very well Mind. https://www.verywellmind.com/constructive-vs-destructive-anger-in-ptsd-2797523

van Dijke, A., Ford, J. D., van Son, M., Frank, L., & van der Hart, O. (2013, April). APA PsycNet. Psycnet.Apa.Org. https://psycnet.apa.org/buy/2012-07231-001

Van Der Kolk, B. (2015). The body keeps the score: mind, brain and body in the transformation of trauma. Penguin Books.

Yogananda, P. (2012). Man's eternal quest. Self-Realization Fellowship.

Yongey Mingyur, Rinpoche, & Swanson, E. (2009). The joy of living: unlocking the secret and science of happiness. London Bantam Books.

Zwemer, W. A. (1984). APA PsycNet. Psycnet.Apa.Org. https://psycnet.apa.org/record/1984-28750-001

著者： Three Initiates. (2012). Kybalion. Bottom Of The Hill Publis.

All images have been sourced from https://pixabay.com

Table of Contents